Goodbye to

ELIPHAZ

LETTING GO OF SIMPLISTIC EXPLANATIONS OF
LIFE, SCRIPTURE & GOD

ROB COYLE

God bless !

RGR

Scriptures quoted are from the NRSV, 1989 unless otherwise noted.

ISBN

www.coyleministries.com

Praise for

Goodbye to Eliphaz

Rob gives us a clear challenge to step back from the "typical". We can't continue offering shallow answers about tragedy and hardship. He challenges us to consider how many pagan attributes we ascribe to God & invites us to see more clearly that God looks like Jesus. This is an important read for anyone serious about knowing what God is like & looking for better answers to life's toughest questions. I highly value Rob's courage to assert that we need to relook at what we may have always thought about life, Scripture, and God.

Eric Reeder
CEO of iLIFE, LLC
President: RISEmovement
Author, Personal Development Coach, Speaker, Thought Leader.
www.ericreeder.life

Rob Coyle knows his way around...around Scripture, church, and the way we think about life. With skill, wit, wisdom, respect for Scripture, and a heart for the hurting, Rob walks us through some of the most vexing stories in Scripture, challenging our "Eliphazic" mindset and making a strong case for a new way of navigating the messiness of life together. This book is a must read for those who are struggling like Job and for those who want to do a better job ministering to Job! Get this book. Enjoy this book.

Don McLaughlin

Preaching Pastor at North Atlanta Church of Christ Author of "Love First" and "Heaven in the Real World"

Contents

Preface

It isn't as easy as some make it seem.

"What isn't easy?" I hear you ask.

Well, life. Life isn't easy.

Life is messy.
Life is rough around the edges.
Life is confusing and hard to understand.

And yet, in all our struggles, confusion, pain and hurting, we long for answers. We want to put the pain behind us, placing it in a nice, easy to understand box. We want to make sense of our circumstances and experiences in a way that coincides with everything else we think we understand about how life works, how Scripture works, and how God works.

Parents get divorced and the children come together to figure out what they did wrong or to determine what role they played in the family misfortune. Believing the family split is their fault, they start finding fault with themselves. At least that makes sense to them when nothing else seems to.

Promotions pass you over at work and you sit back and try to figure out what God is up to, why He didn't want you to move up the ladder and experience success and happiness, but that other person... that other, less deserving, maybe even *immoral* person, is blessed by Him while you sit frustrated and hurt.

Death decides to pay an untimely visit to your loved ones, snatching them away too soon, and you are left wondering why.

Your body is stricken with disease.
Your spouse cheated.
Your children won't speak to you.
Your parents neglect you.

On and on life goes. It's not to say life is nothing but pain and sorrow, (despite what Wesley says.[1]) Life certainly does have moments of joy and happiness. But when it comes to explaining life's darker moments, often the times of joy just add to the confusion.[2]

How can I be so fortunate in my work life, but so cursed in my family life?

---

[1] Princess Bride, "Life is pain, princess"...love that movie.
[2] The book of Ecclesiastes makes this point abundantly clear. Life has beauty, but in the end we all die. Not fair.

Why am I blessed with good health, but I can't seem to find anyone to share my life with?

Why do I sense that the presence of God is actively at work in my life, and yet I can't seem to find employment?

I wish the questions stopped here, but they do not.

Life is too messy for the questions to simply be *only* about the "individual" issues we struggle with on a daily basis.
Life presents us with macro problems as well.

School violence.
Mass shootings.
Terrorism.
Wild fires.
Storms and tornadoes.
Earthquakes and destruction.
Robbery.
Murder.
Abuse.
Disease.

The list is nearly endless. And in this infinite list of woes, we all find ourselves longing to answer one seemingly simple question: Why?

Why is this happening to me... to us... to them?

Or, often, the questions get much sharper. Why is this happening **to us** and *NOT to them... you know, those ever-deserving-of-punishment people over there?*

Why did my child, whom I would gladly die for, die early while our foster system is filled with children whose parents seemingly couldn't care less about what happens to their child, or at least they can't seem to get control of themselves so that they can care for them?

All of these situations, and countless more, force us into asking what are, in my opinion, ultimately impossible questions to answer:
Why?
Why did God do / allow this?

And, one would hope that the sheer weight of these questions, longing to find reasonable answers to life's most painful moments, would give pause to those who might think they have the answers. But my experience tells a different story.

Far too often, there are those around us, perhaps close friends, most often religious leaders, who feel the need to enlighten us when we are in the midst of a physical, emotional or spiritual struggle against life's bleakest forces. They swoop in like paratroopers, armed to the teeth with simple answers to complex questions.

And while the answers might be concise, having an appealing simplicity to them, they fall short when taken into careful consideration.

This is seemingly never more true than when the answers we are given come to us from the Bible and would-be Bible experts.

When answers to life's most challenging questions arise, we often find ourselves in conversation with others in our faith-family who seem to have discovered every answer to every question. And those answers are found in *-dramatic pause-* the **Bible**.

Now, at this point, you may be getting a little nervous about what I am going to say next. So, I will say this. If you are feeling this way, you probably should be. Because what I am about to say may challenge you in a way you have never been challenged before.

The Bible is an incredibly complex book that can be used to say and support a great many, *(and at times contradictory)* things.

Many treat the Bible and its answers for life like an app on your phone.

"Oh, you have a problem? There's a verse for that!"
"Can't find work, I have a verse for that."
"Feeling down and depressed? Here's a book of 'Bible promises' to read… they'll make you feel better."
"Can't figure out where you stand on immigration policy and the government's directive to separate families? I have a verse for that."
"Don't know who to vote for? I have a verse for that."
"Wondering why the hurricane changed direction at the last moment and hit this city instead of that city? You guessed it! I have a verse for that."

"I have verses that explain everything. Just come see me."

It would be easy for this to be humorous *(in fact, I heard many of you laughing irrationally as you read that)*, except for the countless harm this type of thinking and biblical interpretation has done to many who find themselves face-to-face with life's toughest struggles. To those people, simplistic answers often do more harm than good, regardless of the intention, even loving intention, behind the simple answer.

Fortunately for us, the very Bible that gets misused and twisted *(not always on purpose… not all who misuse the Bible are on a mission to hurt you and twist Scripture. In fact, most are not.)* in an effort to find answers to hard questions, warns the faithful follower and Bible student of the temptation to turn the Bible into an "easy answer" book.

It is the Bible that warns us of the danger of trying to make it into an "easy answers for every question" book, written to solve all our questions and concerns.

The Bible is not an app, and the Bible knows it!
The Bible doesn't operate like a GPS system, easily telling us as clearly as possible how to

get from our house to a place we have never been with a "turn here in 300 feet" clarity of speech.

The Bible is not a book designed to supply us with easy solutions to every struggle and doubt we face.

And the funnier *(odder, stranger)* thing about it is that there are times when the Bible appears to be doing just that!

There are parts of the Bible that seem to be crystal clear, with no grey area whatsoever. For those of us who long for simple, clear-cut answers, these passages are favored. Like moths to the proverbial flame, we fly to these passages of Scripture, knowing that they will provide certainty in our moments of *(hopefully)* fleeting confusion.

But, what we will discover, as we consider the topic of the Bible and our simplistic understandings of life, Scripture and God, is that the Bible is less like a step-by-step guide to life and more like a back-and-forth conversation between often opposing perspectives *(if you need this last statement to be explained more fully, then you will just have to read all of this book... gotcha!!!)*.

The Old Testament book of Job will serve as the foundation for all the issues and passages of Scripture we will consider in this book. His story and experiences will serve as the base for everything we talk about, even though the chapters themselves do not focus on Job, but other passages of Scripture.

To sharpen the last point, Job's friends will serve as the metaphoric representation of a way of thinking about life, Scripture and God. One of the three friends will serve as a representative for all three friends as they all approach Job, their bibles and God in a similar, if not identical fashion.

May God bless us as we consider together what it means to say Goodbye to Eliphaz.

Introduction

Eliphaz Spoke Wrongly

The book of Job comes to us from the merry old land of Uz. And Job is living in what could be described as a "garden of God" type of existence.

Life is good (not messy).
Life is smooth sailing (not rough around the edges).
Life is straight forward and easy to comprehend (not confusing at all).

Job is blessed.
And I mean Deuteronomy 28:1-14 blessed.[3]

His fields are producing.
His children are the perfect biblical numbers (3 daughters and 7 sons... perfect).

His livestock is flourishing in a phenomenal fashion as well, also making great biblical math.

And, why might this be so? What is causing God to bless this man as promised by the Bible? Well, Deuteronomy 28 tells us, as does the beginning of Job!

---

[33] I hereby give you permission to read any and all passages of Scripture that are referenced. Any translation you want.

Job is righteous. He is very righteous. To put the cart before the horse, just for a moment, ask Job just how righteous he is and he will tell you. Just read chapters 27-31. This is not a self-righteous, holier than thou, self-perception. It is an account of **who** and **how** Job is. He is "blameless and upright", just as stated in 1:1, 1:8 & 2:3 (in the last two verses, he is called this by God...**place the blue ribbon upon Job's chest!!!**).[4]

Job is such a good, faithful and blameless guy, he makes sacrifices for his 10 children, just in case they messed up. He is a good, good father.

But, like a cheesy, modern day joke, Job's story goes south... fast.

Satan[5], on an apparently routine run with the other "sons of God",[6] has come back from roaming the land, looking for people who have messed up so he can report their lawless deeds and faithless acts to God.

---

[4] I stole this line from comedian, Brian Regan.
[5] "the satan" in Hebrew. A rare term in the Hebrew Bible.
[6] While a complex phrase, it is obvious to me and others that the sons of God referred to here are divine, angelic-type beings who work for and report to God.

In the book of Job, and in other places in the Bible, this is Satan's job. He must have a pretty impressive resume too.

As Satan takes his turn in reporting the goings-on of the people of earth to God, God addresses him and asks him if he took the time to examine Job.

To this, Satan basically says, "What would be the point of that?!! Why would he ever break his relationship with You? You have protected him and built up a fortress of blessings around him. Let him live under the curse of Deuteronomy 28:15 and following and you will see how quickly he turns."

This conversation between God and Satan happens twice. And Job losses everything.

His flocks are taken by his enemies.
His fields are consumed by fire like Sodom and Gomorrah.
His servants are all dead, crushed by the enemies.
A great wilderness wind destroys the home of his eldest son where all his children were eating and drinking, killing them all.

Still Job remains faithful.

Satan then afflicts Job with a very noticeable curse from Deuteronomy. He is stricken with boils from the crown of his head to the soles of his feet.[7]

His wife tells him to "bless God and die!"[8]

Job is sitting in an ash heap, an ancient Gehenna, scraping his cursed boils with broken pieces of pottery, left to weep over the loss of loved ones, possessions and health… all alone.

Three friends hear the news and determine to be by his side… you know, to help. Their names are Eliphaz, Bildad and Zophar. All three represent well-meaning, spiritual companions who, though filled with love for Job, end up allowing their simplistic understandings of life, Scripture and God to guide them to mistreat the man they care about and misspeak about the God they believe in.

SIDE NOTE: Whoever thought that the Bible, because it is old, doesn't have anything to offer a modern people simply hasn't been paying

---

[7] Deuteronomy 28:35

[8] Most translations state "curse", but the Hebrew word is actually "bless", assumed to be used sarcastically.

*attention to Job or a great many other books
of the Bible.*

They sit with him for 7 days (*there's that
number again*) in silence. Make no mistake.
They are there because they care.

Job, in chapter 3, laments the day he was
born as sorrow surrounds him like a dark
cloud and sickness drags his body ever nearer
to Sheol, the place of the dead.[9]

It is now, as Job concludes his lament, that
Eliphaz and friends decide it is time to help
their hurting friend get back on his feet. The
moment has come for him to return to his
former glory. People need to respect him
again like they once did. Job 29 tells us of
how his life used to be, a life blessed and
highly honored, and they want him to get
back to that type of life. The one where God
obviously loved him and was pleased with
him.

So, they do what any good, Bible believing
friend would do. They try to get him to
confess his sin -whatever it might be- so that

---

[9] See the book, "Shades of Sheol" by Johnston for an in-
depth study of this.

God can remove the curse and bring back the blessings.

In chapter 4, Eliphaz can no longer hold his tongue. He speaks to Job, first recognizing how Job used to be righteous; but he does so only as a lead in to how something in Job's life must have changed. To Eliphaz, it is more than obvious that Job has allowed sin to enter his life and destroy everything.

When you think like Eliphaz, you have no choice but to believe that even a man like Job must have done something wrong. This thinking is reinforced when you believe you have Scripture on your side.

In 4:7, Eliphaz makes this remarkably biblical observation. "Think now. Who that was innocent ever perished? Or where were the upright cut off?"[10]

In other words, "Job... we all know how God operates. We all know, you included, what the Bible says. You don't live under a curse for no reason. The faithful do not suffer like this. The righteous do not experience the type of things you are experiencing. This type of

---

[10] Psalm 37:25

punishment is reserved for sinners.
Therefore, you are a sinner. Fess up and get
back to the good life!"

And, for approximately the next 29 chapters,
Job finds himself making a defense of his own
life and character.

Let's summarize a little, shall we?

Chapters 4-5: Eliphaz says God is punishing
Job so he can repent of whatever atrocity he
committed to deserve such treatment.
Chapter 6-7: Job disagrees.

Chapter 8: Bildad *(in true Eliphaz fashion)* tells
Job his children are dead because they were
sinners. He tells Job he has forgotten God
and this is why these things are happening.
This makes life understandable and Bildad is
throwing down that biblical knowledge like a
champ.
Chapters 9-10: Job says it simply isn't so and
he wishes he had a lawyer who could take his
case to the highest court known to man: the
heavenly court.[11] But Job feels that he has no
one.

---

[11] In the beginning of Job, the meeting of God with the
sons of God is often seen as the divine counsel.

Chapter 11: Zophar (*another Eliphaz disciple*), approaches Job and makes it known that the case against Job is worse than they thought. Job is living in denial and is simply refusing to recognize his sin. He calls for God to speak and set Job straight. He also says that, due to Job's lack of honesty, Job is receiving a lighter sentence from the heavens than he deserves. Oh… and he tells Job he is basically an idiot and that a man like him will be considered wise when pigs fly.[12]

As you might have guessed by now, Job isn't having it. He insists, for the rest of the book, in the face of his critics, the friends who have a certain understanding of how life, Scripture and God work, that they are wrong.

He calls them "miserable comforters".[13] Over and over again, he proclaims that he is innocent despite their proclamations of just how easy it is to see what is going on.

Eliphaz and company have grabbed ahold of a way of thinking that allows them to make life make sense. The Scripture is clear regarding

---

[12] See Job 11:12
[13] Job 16:2

situations like Job's. The clarity of Scripture makes the actions of God easy to determine.

Job has sinned and God is punishing him.

There are plenty of passages of Scripture that support this, as we will look at in the next chapter.

The great part about Job (or "a great part" about Job) is that at the very outset of the book, every reader already knows just how wrong Eliphaz and those with him are!

Unlike Eliphaz (and Job, actually), we get a peek behind the curtain. We, the readers and listeners, already know that Job has done nothing wrong. There is something happening in the life of Job that challenges all their current, simplistic understandings about life and God and Scripture. They don't have any passages that will help them understand what is going on. And, as Job does throughout the book, he simply turns elsewhere, outside the Bible, in his struggle to know what is happening and why.

They ask him if he has ever seen the wicked prosper, because the Bible is clear that the wicked do not. Job takes one look around and says, "Yep, and if you weren't so blinded by your immature understandings, you would see them too!"

They tell Job that he is suffering the plight of a sinner. Perhaps before his brush with death, he would have agreed with them, but now he knows better. His experience and honest approach to his situation force him to know better... because he knows, as God had already recognized at the outset, that he has done nothing wrong. God isn't punishing him for some sin. God isn't trying to teach Job a lesson nor is He refining him like gold through the fire. The point of Job's suffering has nothing to do with Job. It has everything to do with understanding that our faithfulness to God is not a pursuit of blessings and an avoidance of curses.

Our service and love of God must run deeper than that. And our understanding about how God works and how Scripture works in our lives cannot be limited to a "passage here" and a "verse there" mentality. As Job finds out in chapters 38-41, God is bigger than that.

In the end of the book of Job, God has these words for Eliphaz.[14]

*"My **wrath** is kindled **against you and against your two friends**; for you have not spoken of me what is right, as my servant Job has."*

Eliphaz had spoken wrongly about God, even though he had scriptures to back up his claims. God's anger was kindled against Eliphaz, not Job. Job, though seemingly relying solely on logic and an honest self-perception, spoke rightly.

When we say Goodbye to Eliphaz, we are letting go of our simplistic understandings of how life works. We are letting go of easy answers to difficult questions. We are saying goodbye to a way of thinking that refuses to consider all the facts, even facts that stand outside the Bible, like the fact that Job was innocent despite all of the preconceived notions that only sin can cause suffering.

We are also recognizing that, often, the conclusions we draw in an attempt to make life and God make sense are even more

---

[14] This is the reason I chose Eliphaz as the representative of simple and immature ways of understanding life, Scripture and God.

absurd than the conclusion *(and in Job's case, the reality)* that God and Satan are playing poker with his life.

Eliphaz represents a mindset that, while attractive as it offers easy solutions, can be harmful. Job was hurt by the behavior, attitudes and actions of his friends. The people who should have been of great comfort to him ended up making matters worse.

It may be that we walk around with an Eliphaz mindset. It is possible that we interpret our own lives, the lives of our friends, the lives of our church family, our communities, our nation and our world through an Eliphaz-like understanding of life. Perhaps we are quick to make the call that this tragedy or that suffering is due to some breach of faith with God. Job teaches us that making sense of life just isn't that easy.

I mean, who would have guessed, without chapters 1 and 2, that Job was suffering due to a heavenly wager between God and Satan? No one!

And that is the point. There are things in life that happen that are simply outside our ability to understand, and our often black and white, stark attempts at explaining them harm the ones we love and speak wrongly about God. It is time to say Goodbye to Eliphaz.

In Matt Schlimm's wonderful book, "This Strange and Sacred Scripture", he points out that the Bible can often be better understood as a conversation between opposing ideas. In chapter 9, titled "The Truth is Many Sided", he imagines a conversation between Ruth and Ezra. If you haven't read this book, you should. The conversation imagines Ruth reprimanding Ezra for tearing families apart due to the joining of Israelites with foreign women. Both Ruth and Ezra have valid points to be made, but they are opposed to one another in the points that they are making. It is a delightfully imaginative portrayal of how I think Job works. In a way, it is a beautiful picture of how the entire Bible works.

The book of Job provides us with an alternative perspective on how we understand life and its many complexities. It shows us a conversation between those who believe that they have it all figured out and those who are unable to see it the same way.

In the end, the certainty asserted by Eliphaz falls short.

It is time to say goodbye.

CHAPTER ONE

Uzzah Had it Coming

The date was January 12, 2010. At 4:43pm, the small island of Haiti was struck by an earthquake that would lead to massive losses of life and property.

According to CNN[15], 220,000 to 300,000 people died as a result. Another 300,000 people were injured. 1.5 million people were displaced and the estimates to repair the damage that had been done totaled over $13 billion.

In the face of such loss, sorrow and despair, the world responds. News anchors flood the tiny island, gathering up personal stories from those who survived the tragic event. Video footage consumes the news channels, showing gruesome images of the damage that had been inflicted.

In the midst of the pain and utter sense of loss, one would expect the church's most vocal and visible leaders to take a stand and

[15] https://www.cnn.com/2013/12/12/world/haiti-earthquake-fast-facts/index.html

speak peace into the turmoil. And, many did just that.[16]

But just one day after the horrific tremors shook that little country, at least one highly vocal and visible Christian spokesperson decided it was time to get to the root of the problem.

Pat Robertson, anchor on the Christian news show, "The 700 Club", representing what is for a great many a mainstream Christian voice, speaks these words of understanding (or misunderstanding) into the situation:

"They [the Hattians] said we will serve you [the devil] if you'll get us free from the French. True Story. And so the devil said ok, it's a deal. And they kicked the French out. You know, the Haitians revolted and got themselves free. But ever since, they have been cursed by one thing after the other, desperately poor." (explanation of characters mine)

Mr. Robertson believes that the poverty they had experienced for generations and the earthquake of 2010 was a direct result of a

---

[16]

http://www.pbs.org/wnet/religionandethics/2010/01/15/january-15-2010-haiti-earthquake/5485/

pact with the devil that was made as they fought against the French for their freedom and independence.

Now, it needs to be stated that Pat isn't happy to report this explanation. In fact, he makes this statement while also attempting to raise funds to help the people in Haiti (see video here).[17] His statement in no way shows that he doesn't care or is unconcerned with the plight of the people. He is not saying, "You made your bed, now sleep in it!" He is saying something else. It is unfair for people to take his statement and bend it to make **him** look like the devil. This is simply not true.

Pat Robertson is making a revelation, but it isn't really about his character. Actually, he is revealing, quite awkwardly but openly, a way in which many people approach life, Scripture and God. Eliphaz has set up shop in his mind.

When confronted with a tragedy, his impulse *(and often, ours)* is to find a means by which to explain what happened.

---

[17]

https://www.youtube.com/watch?time_continue=28&v=S5nraknWoes

"Why did God do this?"
Or,
"Why did God allow this to happen?"

The idea that God would cause or allow an earthquake to kill and displace so many without cause is unfathomable. We believe that there has to be a reasonable explanation for everything. Everything happens for a reason!!![18]

"Perhaps God is punishing them for some horrific, God-forsaking moment in their history. Maybe they are under a curse of some sort. Maybe they made their bed with the devil and now they are suffering the consequences of sleeping with Satan. Sin gives birth to death, after all."

"Besides, everybody knows that God blesses those who are faithful to him, so the fact that they are living in poverty and suffering the destructive forces of nature are an indicator that something has gone wrong in their moral character. Right, *RIGHT?!*"

---

[18] This statement is said and believed by many. It is another simple explanation that falls short, even if saying it to ourselves gives us immediate comfort.

Fortunately *(or, unfortunately depending on how you look at it)*, we are not the first people to deal with these situations, questions, doubts and easy explanations. For thousands of years, people all over this planet have struggled to understand this life we live. Ancient cultures, and modern for that matter, considered what we call "forces of nature" to be gods. They had a god for everything.
Gods for the harvest.
Gods for reproduction.
Gods for war.
Gods for the ocean.
They had sun gods, moon gods, star gods, storm gods, lightning gods… you name it. There was a god for everything.

And, each of these gods needed to be appeased or appealed to in some way. In the ancient near east, the gods they believed in and worshipped were easily offended. It didn't take much to make them lash out at humanity.

In the Epic of Gilgamesh, the gods are frustrated at the level of noise the humans are producing, making it impossible for the gods to rest. The gods send a flood to destroy all of humanity, but one man is saved by one of the goddesses as she determines that, despite the disturbance, they still need humans to give them food to eat (i.e., sacrifices were the food of the gods).[19]

The mindset of the ancient people was simple. Floods come = the gods are angry with us.
Fields not producing? The gods are angry at us.
Can't have children? The gods are angry.
What's that? You lost a battle in war that you are pretty sure you should have won easily? The gods are angry.
There's a famine in the land? The easiest explanation is that the gods are angry.

The opposite is also true.

Everything is going your way? Life is good? Family is doing well? Livestock is continuing to flourish? The seasonal rains are continuing, uninterrupted, as they water the ground? Again, it isn't difficult to understand why!!! The gods are happy with you, your people, your culture, your society, your sacrifices and

---

[19] This is the Babylonian story that has a section very similar to the Bible's "Flood of Noah" account. Also see Psalm 50:12-15

your land. If it were otherwise, you would most certainly be suffering loss until you changed your god-angering ways.

Now, at this point you may be thinking, "Well, sure. PAGANS believed that the gods, life and sacred texts operated this way. **BUT NOT THE PEOPLE IN THE BIBLE!!!** The people and stories that fill its pages are different. They have a better understanding of life and God!"

I wish that were true. Well, it actually is true in part... but it isn't *always* true. While there are people in the Bible who seem to get it, there are a great many who simply do not. It actually seems to me that a majority of the people in the Bible don't get it. Even people who we think should get it, often don't. They are as plagued as Pat Robertson as they attempt to make life, Scripture and God make sense.

A great example of this *(don't worry. We will deal with plenty more, later)* comes to us from 2 Samuel 6. It is in this story, that we find that the ark of the covenant is located in the house of Abinadab, a man who lived on a hill. King David wished to return the ark to its proper location, so he had a new cart constructed on which to transport it. The sons of Abinadab were driving the cart from the top of that hill to Jerusalem so that the ark could be in the tabernacle, as prescribed by the law.

As they went, the men (over 30,000 of them), led by king David, danced, played music and sang praises to God with all their might and a good time was had by all…

UNTIL…

The oxen that were pulling the cart stumbled and the ark was shaken. Out of an impulse (*a completely understandable impulse I might add*) a man named Uzzah reached out his hand to stabilize the ark. And, he died, right there. He died, because the law was very clear about who cannot touch the ark of the covenant (Numbers 4:1-15).

Now, this had to be an amazingly difficult event to understand. After all, they are attempting to put the ark back in its rightful place. The crowd (*think charismatic, mega-church on steroids*) is worshipping God joyously. They even made a brand-new cart to carry it on.

Then, out of nowhere, the ark begins to wobble and a man dies in an attempt to stop the ark from falling.

So, they do what any normal, ancient near eastern person would do. They begin to determine why God would "breakout"[20] against Uzzah. It is said that David is angry because God broke out against Uzzah. It also states that David is afraid of God. Understandable, right? Wouldn't you be angry and afraid?

Before we go further, I want to deal with the simple answer that has been given as to why God would kill Uzzah. The answer I heard growing up *(perhaps you did too)* is that they were carrying the ark incorrectly. Per the law of Moses, it was to be carried by Levites with poles. They had disobeyed God's instruction and He had no choice but to breakout against him. Uzzah had it coming!

See! A clear, easy answer to a difficult passage and event.

---

[20] In verse 8, it is stated that they called the place this occurred, "Perez-uzzah". This means "God broke-out against Uzzah".

As is pointed out in the book, "The Lost World of the Israelite Conquest", the story isn't so easily understood and explained.

First, nowhere in the text does the Bible tell us that God broke out because they carried the ark incorrectly. Read it twice if you like, but the fact is that this easy explanation *(the one that might appease our modern, answer seeking ears)* just isn't there, no matter how much we might want it to be. In fact, this answer is completely unsatisfactory. As the story unfolds, we find that they continue to transport the ark to another location, supposedly on the same cart it was already on. No one else dies on that journey. God doesn't cause the cart to wobble once more to show them that they haven't learned their lesson. All is well, all the way to the home of Obed-Edom the Gittite.

Interestingly enough, the story actually tells us why David believed God had broken out and killed Uzzah. David believed that God didn't want the ark to be under his care!!! David blames himself and has the ark taken to another location, a location **not prescribed** by the law.

Bizarre, right?
Crazy, no?

Where did David get this idea that God didn't want him to care of the ark? How does David make the determination that God has changed His mind about where the ark should be located? We have no idea. It is simply how David interpreted the situation.

The story then gets even weirder. As the ark is at Obed-Edom's house, he is being blessed richly. He and his house are experiencing what they can only say is the blessing of God as the ark resides in his home.

Again, this makes no sense. The ark isn't where God told them to put it and stands in clear violation of the law. And yet, the person who is in "unlawful" possession of the ark is said to be blessed by God. *How can this be?*

When David hears about the blessings Obed-Edom is experiencing, he has the ark brought to Jerusalem. Is he jealous that Obed-Edom is getting the blessing that should be for the king? Maybe. This wouldn't be the worst thing David could be accused of doing.

Perhaps there is another explanation as to why David gets the ark. This explanation fits the pattern of thought David had already developed and relied upon. If God is blessing Obed-Edom, it is because **God is no longer angry** and is no longer breaking out against people. God has calmed down and is back to His blessing ways. The blessing was the sign to bring the ark back.[21]

The Bible is unclear as to how the ark was returned. It sounds as though they are now carrying it properly, but the text is unclear.[22] What is clear is that David is still somewhat afraid of God, even if it is now being carried as prescribed.

How do we know David is still driven by fear? Keep reading.

In verse 13, the Bible tells us that after 6 steps, David made a sacrifice to God. The wording in English isn't very clear. It is actually after **every** 6 steps a sacrifice is made.

---

[21] Chances are these two reasons both played a role as to why David decided it was time to get the ark. They are not mutually exclusive.

[22] The account in 1 Chronicles 13-15 tells us it is carried correctly.

But why would David do this?

Moses never commanded a sacrifice be made every six steps. In fact, he didn't command a sacrifice be made at all as the ark is moved from place to place.[23]

Even if Moses had commanded such a thing, David certainly wasn't the one who was to be offering the sacrifice. He wasn't a priest or a Levite. He was of the tribe of Judah. But throughout the story, David makes everything about himself. *He* wears the priestly garments, though of the tribe of Judah, not the tribe of Levi. *He* makes the sacrifices. *He* pitches the tent in Jerusalem upon their arrival. *He* leads the dancing and singing. *He* makes sacrifices once the ark is in the tent.

So, what drove this action on David's part?[24] What drove David to implement sacrifices and joy-filled, charismatic worship?

---

[23] Just imagine how much longer the wilderness wanderings would have been?

[24] Again, worth noting that the version of this story in 1 Chronicles does attempt to clear out some confusion, but we are still left with many unanswered questions. The conflicting information found between 1 Samuel -2 Kings and 1 &2 Chronicles is well documented as well. It is no surprise that the accounts are somewhat different with

As with most questions like this, we do not know for certain. But, all indicators point to David wanting to make sure that, as the ark is brought under his care, God doesn't breakout again. In order to do that, David decides to make plenty of sacrifices along the way. He and his men dance and sing with all their might, once again, in an attempt to not make God angry, and He seems like He might get angry pretty easily.

Or worse, he implements sacrifices in order to appease a possibly already angry God. David appears to be fully convinced that God had been or currently was angry with him. Every decision he made and every action he took was done in an effort to not let God breakout again.[25]

As stated earlier, the Bible is filled with stories where people are trying to make sense of life, Scripture and God. This story is no exception.

---

one offering explanations and details that the other does not.

[25] "The Lost World of the Israelite Conquest" has a great chapter on this story. It is a difficult book to get through, but well worth it.

And every simple explanation that can be found is met with even more questions.

David approached this situation in an Eliphaz-like fashion, with answers to all of life's complexities. Why did Uzzah have it coming? Why did this happen? David seemed to know, but he was wrong.

It is a dangerous thing to approach life as Eliphaz. He, too, claimed to have all the answers. He seemed to know all the mysteries. He actually thought he could see behind the curtain, understanding life, Scripture and God in a way that Job simply couldn't. And his (mis)understandings led him and his friends to become the most miserable comforters Job had ever met. His way of understanding the difficulties of life led him to make life even more problematic. The presupposition that God blesses only the good and curses only the bad made him ignore the obvious truths that were right in front of his face. Bad things happen to good people and wonderfully good things happen to the worst of people.[26]

Finding a verse of the Bible here and there that says otherwise is being unfaithful to Scripture, unfaithful to others and unfaithful to God.

There comes a point in the life of a believer when we need to let go of the always clear-cut answers that have for too long guided our lives. Our simplistic understandings often lead us to say and do more harm than good. Earthquakes hit and we blame 200-year-old pacts with the devil and how God has finally gotten around to punishing them.
Loss of property, health and life is attributed to some past sin committed or even a familial curse we believe is being lived under.

A man dies as the ark is being transported and we blame it on the wrong type of vehicle or people who are carrying it, stating that God killed him because they didn't use poles or proper people. Or, as David thought, God did this because He doesn't want the ark to be under his care.

---

[26] The longest reigning King of the ancient Jews was Manasseh who is credited with being the worst king they ever had.

None of these explanations speak rightly about God. None of the answers rightly use Scripture. None of them understand how life works.

Eliphaz got it wrong. His friends with him also spoke wrongly about God, even though it seemed that Scripture was on their side. And we can get it wrong too. In fact, we are bound to get it wrong.

Perhaps a better approach to life is to say, "I'm not sure why this is happening to me (or them). I don't know if God is causing or allowing this for any reason I will ever understand. And, though it looks as though a cloud has covered my life and showered me with curses of biblical proportions, I am not so proud as to think I can figure everything out. I will not curse God and die, nor will I blindly believe that everything bad that happens to me is my fault or can be attributed directly to some sin of mine or of others. Life isn't that easy. Scripture isn't that easy. Understanding God and His plans and His ways isn't that easy."

It is time to say Goodbye to Eliphaz.

Time to let him go his way, taking his harmful and overly simple answers with him.

CHAPTER TWO

Chemosh, Human Sacrifice & Strange Moabite Victory

The story of Uzzah is not the only one that represents the ancient struggle to make sense of this life and how we understand the "why" behind the events that take place.

As noted, much of what we see in the ancient world is an attempt to understand what God, *(or the gods)* is up to based on a clear but mistaken understanding of who God is or who the gods are.

Ancient peoples understood life to work via a certain, often predictable, pattern. This pattern was extremely clear, being both easy to identify and follow.

A man touches the ark and dies, it is easy to find the reason why and work towards remedying the situation. Change the mode of transportation to be a stricter following of the law. That should do the trick. But then, quite oddly, not follow other parts of the law... or add to the law by performing uncalled for sacrifices along the way... and all is well.

All these actions were taken due to the ancient mindset *(or not so ancient, as bad luck would have it)* that interpreted the world through the filter of an angry God who breaks out against His people for one infraction, but apparently not for other infractions. In other words, make God happy, maybe even impressing Him by loud singing, dancing and the sweet smell of sacrifice on the way.

It is this certainty and clarity of understanding that drives many to say and do such Eliphaz type things.

In the not so distant past, there was a school shooting that rocked our culture. Unfortunately, these types of events seem to happen more and more often, leaving those who remain to try and figure out why this happened or why God allowed this to happen.

In the wake of this horrible tragedy, the Social Media feeds were calling for all sorts of actions to be taken.

Gun control must be discussed.
Mental health and access to weapons must be addressed.
Bullying and oppression of others needs to be fixed.

The list of topics and things being discussed seemed endless, at least as endless as the need to address them.

As might have been expected, though I wish it weren't, there were still others who had other ideas as to what needed to be fixed in order to prevent this type of activity in the future.

The blame was laid at the feet of God being kicked out of schools.

No prayer in school (*sanctioned school prayer*) is a sign that God is no longer allowed in school. And if the government kicks God out, then God won't be there to protect those kids when evil comes marching through the door with guns.

Not being allowed to pray in school is considered to be just one sign of our godless society and how far we have fallen. We also have Darwinian evolution being taught and creationism being shut out. Again, God has been left outside the schoolyard fence, forbidden to enter. Should we be surprised by the wickedness that invades us when we shut Him out?

Of course, this way of thinking only goes so far. Many of the kids who were killed were faithful followers of Jesus. Though teachers weren't allowed to lead children in prayer, the children have not been restricted of this right. God is still there.

And though evolution is indeed being taught, with many schools not allowing for alternate views, it is worth noting that there are great many believers in God who also believe God used evolution as the mechanism by which all things were created.[27]

In other words, many of the signs we claim show our godless, downward spiral toward hell are not necessarily so. And while we may not, like David, claim that God has broken out against us due to our actions, we do hear (or perhaps even think ourselves) that God has allowed this to happen for the reasons listed.

It is our view of life and how it intersects with Scripture and God that can lead us to such conclusions. In this way, we aren't completely different from those who have gone on before us, hoping to look at life's worst moments, and even life's best

---

[27] This isn't a book on this debate. This is just a simple recognition that for many, there is nothing anti-God about evolution, even if you do not subscribe to the theory.

moments, and filter them through the "What did we do to deserve this?" filter.

David may have looked at Obed-Edom and thought, "Why should he be getting the blessing? He doesn't deserve it!"

After all, this is how he viewed the world. "Why did God strike Uzzah?" and "Why are the blessings now flowing over there and not here?" are reasonable questions to ask and the conclusions he reached are also reasonable when you understand life and God the way he did.

As I stated at the beginning of this chapter, the tragic story of Uzzah isn't the only example we see in the Bible of an ancient understanding of life and God.

Eliphaz can be found in many, many places.

2 Kings 3 brings us our next example of another Eliphazic[28] event from the life of God's people, this time while under the rule of king Jehoram, who ruled when Elisha, Elijah's successor, was the prophet in the land.

---

[28] I know this isn't a word...but work with me people.

The king of Moab, named Mesha, decided he was tired of being ruled over by Israel, especially now that Ahab and Jezebel were out of the picture. Obviously, Jehoram isn't too pleased with the decision made by Mesha to rebel against him and God's people.[29] He rallies his allies from Judah *(king Jehosaphat)* and Edom to wage war against this insurrectionist farming king, Mesha.

Jehoram even gets the reluctant blessing from Elisha and is told by God's prophet that Jehoram will pursue Mesha and defeat him. Elisha even tells him that pools of water will appear, even though there is no rain, as a sign that God will give them victory over Moab. And, so they are off to defeat their foes.

And they do, for a while. Actually, it is looking really bad for Mesha and his people. At first, Mesha believes that his enemies have turned on each other as the new pools of water look like blood in the sunlight *(remember, these pools of water were empty the last he looked,*

---

[29] It should be noted that Mesha isn't quite the king you might picture when you think about kings. He is a sheep breeder, forced by Israel to bring them animals and skins from his herds. A lot of them. You should probably read this story. It only takes a minute.

so what else could it be but the blood of his now feuding enemies?). He was wrong. Severely wrong. Mesha and his men were forced to flee before the people of God, just as Deuteronomy had described *(you remember this passage, correct?).*

So far, so good. Right?

The godly coalition decimated the land and wells of the Moabites. They tore down their walls as they chased them in what is sure to be a certain and decisive victory.

Mesha and his Moabite men are cornered, trapped and desperate, hiding behind the only walls that remain. As the walls began to fall due to the attack of Israel, Judah and Edom, Mesha made a final, last ditch effort in order to avoid certain defeat and death.

He took his oldest son, the one who was to take over when he dies, and offered him up as a burnt sacrifice on the wall to his god, Chemosh.

Inexplicably, after his human sacrifice, the tides turn against Israel, Judah and Edom, despite the words of the prophet and the pools of water that formed with no rain. The

Bible tells us that great wrath came upon Israel, Judah and Edom and they fled, returning to their own land.

No other explanation follows, which is a complete bummer because I have questions.

We are left with a mysterious story about Mesha, human sacrifice and the strange victory (or at least avoidance of defeat) by Mesha, the sheep breeding king of Moab.

Noteworthy is the fact that the longest Iron age inscription that we have from that region accounts for the skirmishes that Moab and Israel had with one another and how their god, Chemosh, had given them multiple victories over Israel, though the specific account from 2 Kings 3 isn't found.[30]

What are we to make of this story? What would Eliphaz make of this story?

This is one of the most difficult stories from which to draw conclusions. Even more baffling is how this story ever made it in the

---

[30] Paker, Simon, "Stories in Scripture and Inscriptions", Oxford University Press, 1997. As to be expected, the Moabite accounts show their god, Chemosh, giving them multiple victories.

Bible to begin with! One would think that a story where human sacrifice to a foreign god is successful would have been understandably left out.

But, here it is, leaving us to read it, scratch our heads and ask unanswerable questions. Questions like:

Did the human offering really work?
Was the prophet Elisha actually wrong?
(maybe he was just being sarcastic... setting them up to fail with his "thus saith the Lord" lead in.)

To these and a great many other questions, we must simply state that we do not know for certain.

It appears that for the people of Israel, the "calamities" the befell them were understood as a direct result of the offering that Mesha made to his god, Chemosh. The story seems to connect these dots with no explanation given. In fact, the story teller and composer of this event do not even sense that people would want to have an explanation.

But, why not?

Why doesn't the author anticipate our questions that long for clear and decisive answers? Why isn't the writer able to see the obvious problems inherent in a story like this?

Again, with stories as old as this one, you can never be too sure. But I would offer up at least one insight, one that is very similar to what we already saw David do with the ark and Uzzah.

The story assumes that those who read it already have an ancient world view where sometimes other nations and their gods are able to overcome Israel and its one, true God. This is just how their world works, folks. The Israelites seemed to believe that it was entirely possible that, whatever the calamities were that overtook them as they were on the verge of complete and utter victory, they were due to the crazy sacrifice Mesha offered up as he set his son ablaze on the wall. His sacrifice was understood to not only appease Chemosh who seemed to be against Moab until that point, but also to invigorate him with the energy to drive back the enemies of his people, the people of God.

Now, I would venture a guess that 100% of the people reading this right now do not believe that this is what happened. You do not believe that the prophet Elisha gave a false prediction or that Chemosh, even for a moment, was able to defeat the Israelites as they operated under the power and authority of God Himself.

So, what do we do? What do we say?

We say this.
Life is messy and complicated. Some things have no easy explanation and no one, not even biblical authors, are able to fully see behind the curtain and observe what is actually going on, despite the clarity with which they speak. Even despite the passages of Scripture they may quote. As we will take a look at in a future chapter, even Satan is able to, and does, quote Scripture without changing a word or a context, and yet the passages he speaks will be corrected by Jesus.

The Eliphaz within us wants to jump in and "tell everyone" what is actually happening.

Eliphaz can't remain silent any longer or accept the fact that life is full of painful mystery that doesn't always fit into the little boxes that we create to try and make every facet of life make sense.

Thinking again about the story of Job, had Eliphaz said, "I know what is going on. Obviously, God and Satan have some sort of heavenly wager going on and you, Job, are stuck in the middle of it.", we *(and everyone else)* would think his idea was absolutely absurd. Ridiculous. Unbelievable!

And yet that is what many of our attempts look like when we approach life as Eliphaz. Our thoughts of, "bring prayer back in school… that'll put an end to school violence" are as far-fetched as deals being struck by Satan and God.

The truth is that we do not know such things. And even when it seems that we have discovered the direct cause/effect answer, more often than not, when it comes to life, Scripture and God, we have not. Instead, we find ourselves running the risk of not speaking rightly about God, just as Eliphaz did.

CHAPTER THREE

Red Heifers & Sabbath Confusion

Ah, the good old days.

By that I mean really, really old days.
Moses days. Aaron days. Miriam days.

Back when life was simpler. Back when living
for God and knowing you were doing a good
job was, well, just easy to know.

I mean, they had this list of easy-to-
understand "dos and don'ts" to guide them.

What it must have been like to live in a simple,
uncomplicated world?! A world where
everything was just so black and white. A
world where no one ever had a question as to
what was the right and wrong thing to do.

"What type of offering does God want?"
Easy. A blameless and pure one. No defects.

"Uh oh. It is Saturday and there is some work
that needs to be done. Can I get to work? It is
really important."
*Umm, no. God rested on the 7th day and told us
to do the same. It can wait… and you should
really plan a little better.*

See? Life was simpler. Easier. And, it was
easier to know if you were doing it right or
wrong.

"How?" you ask.

Well, the Scripture tells you. Deuteronomy 28 says it as clearly as anywhere.

Verses 1-14: You know you are doing it right because you will be blessed. And by blessed, it means rich. Abundant fields, flocks and numerous children. Enemies? Not to worry. They will drop off like flies or stand in fear of you.

Oh, and it will rain when it is supposed to, allowing your fields to flourish and make the other nations completely jealous of you.

When this happens, you know you are following God correctly. Health and wealth will overtake you. Sounds good to me! *(and apparently to a great many prosperity gospel preachers and their subscribers... go figure.)*.

But, how do you know you are doing it wrong? How do you know you messed up and have failed to live up to the Law?

Again, pretty clear. And scary.
Very. Scary.

Verses 15-68 paint a pretty clear and stark picture of the fate of those who fail to follow the codes. Honestly, it is depressing to summarize these verses... but here we go:

You will be cursed (like Job). Boils head to toe. Poverty and famine will devastate and devour you. Your enemies will defeat you. Your flocks will die. You won't have any offspring and the ones you already have will be slaves to other nations. And, you will end up eating some of your kids due to hunger. Plagues will make you so pathetic that eventually the nations that might have taken you as slaves won't... because you won't be worth the effort to them.[31]

Now, as drastic and hard-to-swallow as these passages might be, one thing is abundantly apparent: the law was clear and the consequences of obeying or not obeying are equally clear to understand and observe.[32]

And, while we might not be overly anxious to experience the curses, at least we can look

---

[31] I understand that I am using a sarcastic tone, but it should be noted that Ancient Near-East blessings and curses were to be understood as hyperbolic to the extreme. They were also intended to strike fear. Deuteronomy is no exception to this rule.
[32] Is it any wonder Eliphaz seemed to know all the answers?

back on those times and say, "They had it harsh, but they had it simple!"

Wouldn't it be nice to live in a world that is so concise and clear? Wouldn't it be nice to have the mystery of life, Scripture and God all cleaned up and compartmentalized for us?

There is only one problem, and it is a big problem. It turns out that there was nothing simple about living under the law.

As Peter Enns points out in his wonderful *(and easy to read, thank God)* book, "The Bible Tells Me So", the law was far from easy and clear. Often it is downright contradictory.

Here are some examples he brings up.[33]

Are Israelites allowed to keep other Israelites as slaves?
Exodus: Yep, with some clarifying marks about when the male slaves are to be set free.
Deuteronomy: You know it! But, men **and women** slaves can gain freedom.
Leviticus: Nope. Never. No men, no women.

---

[33] Be sure to buy and read this book. You'll be glad you did...probably.
"The Bible Tells Me So", Enns, Peter; Harper Collins, 2014 pages 160-164

Why would you do that? You were already slaves in Egypt!

So much for clarity on what to do and how to do it right.

You might say, "Yeah, well... I bet there isn't any confusion over sacrifices, er, at least Passover sacrifices, right?!"

I'm not sure how to break this to you, but even the instructions on this are not very clear.
Exodus 12: Roast the lamb... do not boil it. This would be a big mistake. A major blunder.

Deuteronomy 16: You're going to have to boil the lamb.

It turns out that staying away from the curses is harder than we might have expected.

Another example... (because examples are fun)

This comes to us from what I call my least favorite Bible story.

It is found in Numbers 15: 32-36. The Israelites are wandering in the desert, having recently[34] received the 10 commands (words) of God from the mountain of Sinai. They had heard the thundering and frightening voice of God list the commands.[35] They had them written on tablets of stone. The command to "do no work on the Sabbath" was there, clear as can be. The consequence for working on the Sabbath was equally clear: death.[36] Rest, or we will put you to rest, permanently.

The story in Numbers 15 tells us about a man who is gathering sticks on the Sabbath.[37] The people find him and bring him to Moses because they do not know what is to be done to him, because they hadn't been told that part, only Moses had. They simply knew that working on the Sabbath was a major no-no. Of course, this doesn't make any sense chronologically. How did they know to find Moses? Why did they think something needed to be done to this stick gatherer?

---

[34] Whatever "recently" means. Sometime between Sinai and the crossing of the Jordan
[35] Exodus 20:8-11
[36] Exodus 31:15
[37] Could also be translated "cutting down trees"

Regardless, Moses should have known what to do, because God had already told him on Mt. Sinai. But he doesn't seem to know.

Though not stated, it appears that Moses approached God and asked Him what was to be done, even though it should have been clear because God had already told him.

If this is the case, I wonder what Moses's confusion was.

Perhaps he questioned whether or not picking up sticks qualified for the death penalty.
Maybe he wasn't sure what qualified as "work".
Maybe Moses started to think to himself, "Does the activity of bringing this man to me today, on the Sabbath, qualify as work? If we stone him today, is that work? Does walking to where the sticks are, like these other people did when they found him, count as a punishable work?"

Honestly, I have no idea. It could be that Moses had no such questions. But, something happened that required God to step in and clear things up.

The story ends with God telling Moses to have the man stoned to death. (*Like I said, not my favorite story in the Bible.*)

My main point is this. Had the law been crystal clear, there would have been no need to hear from God, AGAIN, about what needed to be done. Just take him to Moses and let Moses read from the law what was to be done...assuming this activity of taking the offender to Moses didn't count as work and therefore a clear violation of the Sabbath law.

God had already spoken clearly.
Unless it wasn't clear and they needed additional guidance.

One last example. I promise. And this one, while totally weird, doesn't offend our modern sensibilities the way the last one does, unless you are offended by strange, ancient practices.

Numbers 19:1-22 tells us of a strange ritual performed by the Israelites. It is the sacrifice of the red heifer.

The cow[38] is to be red, without blemish and to have never had a yoke placed upon it. A

---

[38] The Hebrew word simply means "cow".

series of bizarre activities take place by
various priests/men; each of whom become
unclean in the process of doing this ritual.
This requires others to step in and pick up
where the last person left off until the
sacrifice and ritual is completed. You should
take a moment and read this passage, just so
you get a feel for how strange this really was.

Upon your first read, it may seem that,
though bizarre and odd, it is fairly straight
forward. Easy enough to perform. Just make
sure you have enough priests and you are all
set. ***Time to get weird!***

But upon a closer reading, you might start to
see how this ritual is nearly impossible to pull
off. Here are some questions, just to get
started:

What does it mean for a red heifer to have
"no defect" and "no blemish"?[39]
Does one with only three legs work?
What if the hoof is damaged, just a little?
How old does it need to be?
How can one tell if a yoke has ever been on it?
What if it looks perfect, but upon closer
inspection, a person finds a few hairs that are

---

[39] Or any sacrifice for that matter.

not red? Is there an accommodation for this?
If so, how many hairs can be some color other
than red? Are there any colors of hair that are
outright unacceptable no matter how many
there are?

Ugh... and do all the people involved need to
be priests (and must one of them always be
named Eleazar)? Some of the passages
specify "priests"[40] while others simply say
"man".[41]

Not to mention the confusion over who is
clean or unclean and when.[42]

Alas, it turns out that there never were "good
old days". All the thoughts we have had
about how easy life, Scripture and God were
to understand are wrong.

Understanding life has never been easy.
Gaining the blessings and avoiding the curses
was never simple and at times the guess of
one was as good as the guess of another at

---

[40] See verses 3-7
[41] See verses 8-22
[42] https://www.jewishvirtuallibrary.org/red-heifer
See this link for a more detailed account of the issues and
solutions/disagreements the Jewish people have
discussed in their past.

determining whether something was being done rightly or wrongly.

Understanding Scripture, even the law which seemingly should have been clear and simple, was never facile. It required thought. It required the input of others. Answers were never simple to come by. In fact, some questions were answered in different ways by faithful people who wanted nothing more than to be faithful to God.

The Passover lamb issue: some decided to roast **and** boil it, just to be safe.

The Sabbath issues of what to do and what qualifies as work: those issues existed even with Jesus, as we will soon see.

Red heifer problems. It is said that this ritual may have only occurred 7 times in Jewish history *(see link on previous page in footnotes)*. Why only 7 times? Probably because it is so incredibly complex to understand and perform.

And, oddly, we should find great solace in the complexity. It is good to know that people have always struggled and fought to understand life, Scripture and God.

Not only should we find solace, we should also find humility. Eliphaz approached life arrogantly. He believed he had all the answers to life's issues.

"Lost your family did you Job? You are living Deuteronomy 28:15-68, my friend. Repent of your unfaithful ways and get your life together! Haven't you read your Bible?"

Job's response, in summary is this:

"I have read it. I've lived it blamelessly and **you know it Eliphaz**. Your simple answers and simplistic understandings are of no use other than to harm me… and I have been harmed enough already. Something else is going on, but, what it is, I am not sure. Please help me or leave me alone."

When I state that it is time to say Goodbye to Eliphaz, I mean it is time for the church to say goodbye to a way of thinking that doesn't acknowledge the true and real complexities of life. Complexities that can't be addressed with a "verse here" and a "verse there" mentality. Issues that need more than Deuteronomy 28 to guide us.

Because sometimes, just sometimes, Deuteronomy 28 simply doesn't work. It is one passage among a myriad of passages that are to be considered. If Eliphaz got it wrong, we most certainly will as well.

If the book of Job teaches us anything, it is this. Life isn't easy. Scripture isn't easy. And God, often, isn't easy to understand either. It is time to say Goodbye to Eliphaz.

CHAPTER FOUR

Zelophehad Had No Sons

It is entirely likely that you have never heard of this man, Zelophehad, from the Bible.

Not to worry. This isn't really your fault... *(well, it kind-of is,)* but let's be nice and say that it isn't. His story is buried in that ever-loved-to-be-skipped-over book of the Bible known as Numbers. Not only that, but the beginning of his story and the end is also separated by 9 chapters of stuff that has nothing to do with him. So, yeah. Kind of tough to be familiar with him. But his story is an important one, as you will soon see.

I will tell you at the outset that Numbers is not exactly my favorite book in the Bible. In fact, it contains some stories that downright make me cringe and wish that, whoever put the Bible together, had left some major portions of this work out.

A man is stoned for picking up sticks on the Sabbath *(as we just saw)*. Not so cool, especially considering that no one seemed to agree on what constituted "work".[43] I mean, how was this poor fellow to know that gathering sticks, presumably for a fire, would

---

[43] Numbers 15

earn him the right to be the first to die by stoning due to a Sabbath transgression?

It is in Numbers that God hears the complaints of **hangry** wanderers and feeds them quail, only go turn and curse them as they ate the food He had provided to punish them for their complaining. The punishment was death, and they were buried there because they couldn't control their cravings.[44]

Yes, this is not exactly a book I go to when I want to feel all warm and fuzzy inside. When a speaker gets up and says, "God is good... all the time, and all the time... God is good." I admit that the stories from Numbers roll around in my head.

Oh... and let's not forget about the story where serpents killed and afflicted the Israelites due to their whining about there being no food or water *(how dare they)*... or the time when the earth opened wide its mouth and swallowed-up rebels who rose up against Moses and Aaron, not with swords,

---

[44] Numbers 11

but rather with words and questions, sending them *alive* into Sheol, the place of the dead.[45]

It isn't any wonder that you have never heard of Zelophehad, the man who had no sons. By the time you read all of this, you are ready to move on and skip to the "good parts."

However, if you skip over his story, the story of his 5 daughters, then you are missing out on one of the richest stories in the Old Testament *(in my opinion... which is always theological gold in my estimation)*.

Eliphaz and friends would have benefited from knowing and considering this story in Israelite history. Perhaps it would have softened their approach as they watch their dear friend Job suffer endlessly. Keep reading and you will see why.

To provide a little set up, it is important to remember a few things concerning inheritance laws, as this is what the story of

---

[45] I would reference all of these, but maybe you should just read Numbers. Just make sure you are either already in a bad mood, or in such a good mood that these stories couldn't possibly lead you to a dark place.

the daughters of Zelophehad are concerned with.

According to the Law, properties and possessions were to be passed on to the firstborn son of any Israelite family. In fact, the first born was to get a double portion and the remainder was to be divided among the other brothers, if there were any.

According to Deuteronomy 21:15-17, God commanded that this be the manner of distributing wealth and possessions upon the death of the father. This also appears to be the way things were done even before the law had been set in stone (so to speak).

Since this is how God prescribed it, it must be perfect and applicable for any situation or circumstance, right? Otherwise, we get into situational ethics, something that Eliphaz and Deuteronomy seem to have no room for. Humanity doesn't have the right to approach God concerning the law He set in place. As Psalm 19 says, His law is perfect and life-giving.

However, the 5 daughters of Zelophehad must have missed the memo regarding God's perfect law. They believe that they have a case, worthy of consideration, where the law of God is unfair and is in need of amending.

They come together, in Numbers 27, and bring their case before Moses and Eleazar, the priest, as they stand at the entrance to the tent of meeting, or tabernacle. In short, they inform Moses that if the law of God is followed as it is currently written (or stated… we don't know when the other commandments were written down. Only the 10 Commandments (or words) were said to be written on the tablets), they (because they are women with no brothers) will be left destitute and without possessions. In their estimation, this is completely unjust and needs to be addressed.

Now, let's stop for a moment.

On what grounds do these women (or young girls, we don't really know) think that their complaint is going to be well received?

Wouldn't they be afraid that the ground would simply open up and eat them alive? Aren't they afraid the serpents would return? Hasn't the idea crossed their minds that a plague might come and wipe them out? I mean, it's happened before when people thought things were unfair and started mumbling. Why would their case be any different?

But it is here where the story takes an interesting, and possibly problematic, turn for the Eliphaz in our midst and minds.

Moses approached God, like he had when trying to determine what to do with that Sabbath-breaking-stick-gatherer, with the case brought up by these 5 daughters to find out what should be done. God speaks and says, **"the daughters are right. The law, as-is, is unfair to them. Let's modify it."**[46]

God makes an amendment to the law so that any Israelite family that finds themselves in a similar situation as these 5 daughters, can rest assured that they will be treated fairly.[47] God even goes on to cover what would seem to be any other unforeseeable circumstances that might arise, just to cover all the bases. I mean, it is time to get this law right, without further need of modification or alteration!!!

---

[46] Okay. Not word for word, so read the story.
[47] Sidenote: so much for God being a sexist and unconcerned for women. This story says otherwise.

If the story ended here, it would be odd enough. Think about it:

Why did the law of God need amended? Doesn't Psalm 19:7 state that the law of God is perfect? How can something that is perfect need to be changed?

And why didn't God, being God, know that something like this would happen and write it into the law ahead of time? Why does it take 5 daughters to convince Him that things are not as they should be?

And how would Eliphaz feel about all of this, remembering that God said that "the daughters of Zelophehad have spoken what is right."? I mean, Eliphaz is told he has not spoken rightly, so this is kind of a big deal.

But, as I mentioned earlier, the story does not end here. If it had, it would already be odd. But it gets odder.

Skip to chapter 36 of *Numbers (the last section of the last chapter of the entire book ends on this story)*. It seems that the things God decreed in chapter 27 were not entirely perfect. He is going to have to take another stab at it.

Here, another group of people, from the same tribe as these daughters, approach Moses and tell him that it might seem like a good idea to allow these women to get an inheritance, but it isn't without potential pitfalls.

They wonder what will happen if these 5 daughters of Zelophehad marry men from **another** tribe? If they do that, then the land that should belong to their tribe will get transferred to another tribe, effectively robbing all future generations of land and possessions. How can this be fair?

Like before, Moses approaches God and, though unstated, apparently hears from God that the complaint of these people is legitimate. The newly amended law needs an additional amendment, in order to be fair to everyone. He states that the women are to marry from within their tribe, if they decide to marry at all.

And this is how the book of Numbers ends. It ends with the law of God being amended and adapted.

This is HUGE!
This story, spread out and separated in the

book of Numbers, is making a major implication regarding how we understand life, Scripture and God.

For those who approach Scripture believing it to be static and unchanging, Numbers offers up a ginormous theological slap in the face.

The law is not static and unchanging. The word of God is not some "black and white" document that is incapable of accommodating new circumstances.

Apparently, there are circumstances and situations that can arise, causing God's law to need a change in order to be fair.

This, in essence, is Job's approach to life, law and God.

Perhaps there was a time when Job would have looked at life with its varied circumstances and stated, quite matter-of-factly, "God clearly states that you are suffering because of sin. Repent and be blessed." This is the way Eliphaz approaches life and the understanding of God and Scripture.

God said it and that settles it.

But stories like this have a way of dismantling this understanding. These 5 daughters had no legal leg to stand on. The law was against them and they had zero reason to believe that their pleas would be greeted with anything other than, at best, rejection. Or at worst... well, let's not imagine the worst.

However, God doesn't reject them, even in a book like Numbers where God would seemingly **NOT** accept any sort of complaint.

If Eliphaz had been in Moses's place, I believe the story would have ended quite differently.

There would have been no need to approach God. What would be the point of that?!! Eliphaz already had a law to go by and any deviation from it would be sure to incur wrath and punishment. Judging from the looks of Job, it would be best not to question God.

But Job... if Job, after having suffered so greatly for no reason, had been asked about this situation, I imagine he would have acted much like Moses.

He would have brought the case before God, recognizing that, as-is, the law is capable of being unfair and perhaps even cruel.

Why?
Because Job understands that life isn't so
easy to understand. It isn't always nice and
tidy. Not every event can be easily accounted
for and explained, even if you have a scripture
that seems to want to explain it.

This story, the story of the 5 daughters,
represents one of the best ways of
approaching life, Scripture and God. It is as
though Job knew this story and Eliphaz had
never heard of it.

Not everything in life is cut and dry, or easily
explained by a passage here or a verse there.
Life presents us with complex issues that
require wisdom and thoughtfulness.

We can't go around like Eliphaz, blaming
everything on a person's sin or rebellion as
the cause for their plight and heartache. Even
Moses, the great lawgiver, didn't do that.

In fact, the daughters were actually quite
careful to make sure that Moses and Eleazar
knew, back in chapter 27, that rebellion was
not to blame for their situation.

They state, quite emphatically, that their
father was not part of the rebellion that led to

the death of many in Israel. He had simply died and rebellion had no part to play in how they ended up in this unfair situation.

Perhaps the church should take some advice from these daughters. Maybe we should listen more carefully to the voices in the Bible who are said to have "spoken rightly" about life, Scripture and God.

These voices from our Bibles have important lessons to share with us as we struggle to understand our own circumstances and how our lives interact with our sacred texts and God.

Eliphaz stands in need of a dismissal.

CHAPTER FIVE

A Strange Fire (and story) Indeed

Leviticus.

Probably, like Numbers, not your favorite book to read when you decide to sit down and have yourself a time of devotion or reflection.

This book of the Bible, unlike Numbers, isn't filled with hard-to-handle stories. In fact, it only has one event that we would call a "full-blown story". Most of the book is filled with sacrifices and how and when to perform them. This is not exactly what you are hoping to read when you wake up early in the morning to have some quiet time with God.

The first 7 chapters, in fact, speak of nothing other than offerings and sacrifices, how to do them and when. Chapters 8 and 9 deal with the consecration of the priests. It isn't until chapter 10 that we find our first narrative, the kind of thing we hope to read when we pick up our Bibles.

Before we jump in, it is important to note what has happened leading up to the story. By this I mean, it is important to understand a little of how Scripture works.

If you look at the many Old Testament stories that have led up to this moment in Israelite history, you will notice a pattern of sorts. There is a recurring theme that is woven throughout the previous books of the Bible that, if we are paying attention, allow the Levitical story to not take us off guard.[48]

Leading up to Leviticus, the Israelites have been freed from Egyptian slavery. They have been given the law of God at Mount Sinai, and the building of the tabernacle has been completed as prescribed by God to Moses.

Everything is ready.
The freed people of God are now able, at long last, to worship their God and redeemer.
They are set up to succeed.
All obstacles have been removed.

What could possibly go wrong?

Well, as I said, if we are paying attention to the stories that have led up to this event, we should know that something bad is going to happen. Humanity has a way of messing

---

[48] Make no mistake. Leviticus 10 can take you by surprise if you aren't familiar with the recurring theme.

things up, even though God has set us up for success.

Think about it.
Adam and Eve are in the garden of God, Eden. It is a place of great beauty and bounty. Everything they could ever need is there. There is no way they can fail...

The flood of Noah has just ended. God pressed the great "reset button" of His creation and only the righteous have been saved from the destructive deluge. Noah gets off the ark, gets drunk and naked.[49] His son Ham does who-knows-what to him while he is in his tent passed out. A curse is pronounced by Noah on Ham's descendants. It seems that man is still evil, even from youth.[50]

Or, how about when God freed them from Egypt in the book of Exodus, the story that I just referenced? What should have been a moment of great triumph and worship turned out to be a time of great revelry and golden calf worship.

---

[49] Probably in that order, but the original language is unclear...(sarcasm)
[50] Genesis 8:21

Yes, it seems that every time God sets His people up for success, they find a way to mess it up.

Leviticus is no different.

We arrive at chapter 10 with great hopes that, for once, things will go as planned.

The priests have been consecrated. They have waited 7 days at the entrance to the tent of meeting. It is now the 8th day, the new beginning, the new creation moment. The messianic oils have been poured upon them and they are ready to carry out their first sacrifice.[51]

But, as you might have guessed, things don't quite go as anyone might have hoped.

You must imagine the utter excitement as everyone has gathered to worship at the newly constructed tabernacle, only to see things fall apart before their very eyes.

Two of the priests, the sons of Aaron, Nadab and Abihu, take their censers and put the fire inside. The text goes on to tell us that the fire

---

[51] See Samuel Balentine's commentary on Leviticus.

they put in their censers is "strange, alien or unauthorized".

For the record, no one really knows what that means. Whatever the case may be, they seem to have messed it up. We are told in verse 2 (*not even 2 verses in, go figure*) that a fire came out from before the Lord and consumed them.

They are dead.
Burnt to death.
God must be angry.

Moses tells Aaron that this must have been what God meant when He said, "Among those who are near me I will be sanctified and before all the people I will be glorified."[52]

At this point, Moses tries to jump in and handle business. He is certain that God has lashed out and killed these two priests because they have stepped out of line and not obeyed every detail of the law. He takes it upon himself to make sure that this doesn't happen again, because, "who knows? If they mess up again God might just kill everyone!"

---

[52] Lev 10:3

This would be bad.
This should be avoided.

Moses proceeds to tell Aaron and the other two, remaining, sons of Aaron, Eleazar and Ithamar, to carry on as though nothing has happened. If they mourn in the customary way, God will pour out his wrath on the entire congregation. Everyone else can weep and mourn over what God has done, but not them. ***The show must go on.***

Moses even goes as far as to tell Aaron and his sons to eat their portions of the sacrifices, just as the law prescribed.

Yeah. Because I am sure that is exactly what they feel like doing: dinning immediately after the burning of their family.

Before we go on, it should be noted that, though in Numbers, Moses is portrayed as the one who communicates with God and is more understanding (*at least in the case of Zelophehad's 5 daughters*) and in the know regarding God and His will, this is not always the case.

Leviticus shows us a different side of Moses, a more Eliphaz-like or even David-like dimension of his personality that we might not have expected.

Moses starts explaining the situation to everyone because he has in mind the word of God as he understands it. He marches around and asks people to do unreasonable things, based on his understanding.

But Moses was wrong.

You might be thinking, "How do you know Moses was wrong?"

Well, I know he was wrong because the story tells us he was wrong.

While Moses has decided to take matters into his own hands, based on his own understanding of God's word, God is actually communicating with Aaron.

In verses 8-11, God tells Aaron, not Moses, that when performing these priestly tasks, it is best done sober. It seems that Nadab and Abihu died, not because God sent out a flame to consume them, but rather because they were drunk.

Nowhere did God tell Moses that the rituals were to be performed sober. That wasn't in the commands previous, but God saw fit to tell them now.

Why wait until 2 men die to let them in on this secret? Your guess is as good as mine.

Moses, however, is thoroughly convinced that they died because they failed to do everything precisely as God had said. He was intent on making sure that from here on out, no more transgressions would take place.

Don't mourn the loss of loved ones... lest you die.
Don't go outside the tent of meeting... lest you die.
Eat the portion of the sacrifices and offerings as commanded. Make atonement as commanded.

For Moses, failure to do these things will lead to certain death.

It is hard to blame him for feeling and thinking this way. He believes God just killed 2 people for not being careful and precise. It hasn't occurred to him that they were drunk, covered in oil and playing with fire. But I digress.

Moses, at this point in the story, is hovering and trying his best to make sure no more punishments will be dealt out from the divine realm due to disobedience.

Epic fail.

Later in the story, moments later, Moses's worst nightmares come true.

The priests, Eleazar and Ithamar (and Aaron) have disobeyed once again. They didn't eat their portion of one of the sacrifices, even though Moses was pretty clear that they needed to do so. They allowed it to be burned up entirely. This, Moses is convinced, is sure to stir up God's fiery wrath. Moses is angry with them and confronts them as they have undoubtedly doomed them all to destruction by fire.

This is where the story gets even more interesting.

Aaron, like the 5 daughters of Zelophehad, has no legal leg to stand on to defend his actions as he and his sons decided to not eat the sacrifice.

Aaron's logic is not based on what God had said nor on what was prescribed in the law.

The law made absolutely no accommodation for any special circumstances or situations that would allow for him and his sons to not eat their portion.

And yet Aaron responds to Moses with the following words:

"Behold, today they have offered their sin offering and their burnt offering before the Lord, and yet such things as these have happened to me! If I had eaten the sin offering today, would the Lord have approved?"[53]

The Bible tells us that, upon hearing Aaron's complaint/logic, Moses agrees with him.

Nothing else happens.

No fire consumes them.
No plague is sent to kill off these disobedient priests.
No ground opens up to swallow them whole.

The congregants that Moses feared for so fervently were left alone, untouched by the hand of an angry, wrathful God.

---

[53] Lev 10:19

God, it seems, is not as Moses imagined Him to be.
The word Moses received and so desperately wanted to obey did not interact in life as he thought it would.

Moses, like Eliphaz, thought he could explain every occurrence in life, especially the bad ones, with some sort of simple, clear-cut understanding of a passage of Scripture.

Moses was wrong.
Eliphaz was wrong.

It is important to note also that even Leviticus disagrees with what exactly happened that day and why these 2 men died. While chapter 10 tells us that they died due to the use of a strange fire, chapter 16 tells a different tale. When this event is reflected upon later in Leviticus, we are told that these 2 men got too close to the Most Holy Place, causing God to breakout against them.

That doesn't sound like strange fire to me.

I find this disagreement to be encouraging. Not every event can be so neatly and easily accounted for in our lives.

More often than not, bad things happen and we are left completely and utterly incapable of understanding why. We, like Moses, may run around, trying to control everything, but we find that we are powerless to control life's events.

We are equally powerless to explain them.

This truth makes some of us uncomfortable. It made Eliphaz and company uncomfortable. If God can't be predicted and, therefore controlled, then what is to stop them from being consumed with fire or covered head-to-toe with boils?

Our need to explain every hurt in life is deeply connected to our need to avoid pain and pursue blessing. We desire to control the situation and are hopeful that our understanding of Scripture and God will help to avoid life's hurts and bring us to the place of prosperity and pleasure.

But Job tells us that this isn't how life works. Somethings in life are simply inexplicable. Sometimes life happens and there isn't an explanation or reason for it.

We run and rave like Moses in hopes of controlling all future heartaches. We think that because we have what appears to be an explanatory verse, that we can be successful in our endeavor.

But it is futile.

Those 2 men didn't die that day because of strange fire.

Moses tried to avoid further disobedient actions that might incur God's wrath, but his pursuit of perfection failed.

He only thought he knew what had happened and why.

So it is with us, as we go through life, like Eliphaz, or in this case, Moses, thinking we can explain life and avoid pain by using the proper Scriptural metric.

We are wrong. Eliphaz was wrong. Moses was wrong.

This isn't the way life works.
It isn't the way Scripture works.
It isn't the way God works.

CHAPTER SIX

Jesus & Biblical Clarity

Jesus stirred the pot.

In fact, in the gospel of Luke, chapter 4, the very first reading Jesus does at the synagogue in Nazareth nearly gets him killed. He hasn't even started his ministry yet and the first thing he does is show the people in his hometown that they seemingly have no idea what their Bibles say, how to recognize the movement of God in their midst, nor how to approach the Scripture in the way it was meant to be approached.

In this account, Jesus has recently returned from his 40 days in the wilderness, overcoming the tests and trials of Satan.

Before we get into the latter part of Luke 4, it is extremely important to note that the temptation Jesus endures in the beginning of Luke 4, in many ways, isn't even remotely close to what we deal with on a daily basis.

I have never been tempted to turn stones to bread or throw myself off the top of a building in hopes that God would dispatch angels to carry me safely to the ground. This is not my kind of temptation... well, maybe the part about finding a quick and easy way to power and authority would be tempting, but the other two I would have passed with flying colors.

The important detail to note though isn't **WHAT** Jesus was tempted to do, but **HOW** Satan tempted Jesus. Satan's tool of temptation sets the stage for much of what happens in Luke's gospel account.

Satan comes to Jesus twice in an attempt to lead Jesus astray by means of hunger for food or power. These attempts fail miserably and are refuted by Jesus with Scriptural authority.

But, he comes to Jesus last with nothing other than Scripture. Perhaps he thinks that if Jesus loves Scripture so much, he will use it against Him. The same Bible Jesus had cited as a means to defeat the schemes of the devil are now being used by the devil himself!

"If you are the Son of God, throw yourself down from here, [10] for it is written,
'He will command his angels concerning you,
to protect you,' [11] and 'On their hands they will
bear you up, so that you will not dash your foot
against a stone.'" (NRSV)

There you have it folks. Jesus, according to Scripture, should be able to go ahead and throw himself from this temple pinnacle and show once and for all he is who God said he was at his baptism: the beloved son of God.

Of course, you should never listen to Satan, even if he is quoting Bible verses at you.

But, why not?
I mean, *other than the obvious reason that it is Satan*, why not listen? Is it Scripture or isn't it? Doesn't Psalm 91 say exactly what Satan said? **Yes, yes it does.**

Jesus does what he will continue to do throughout Luke. He juxtapositions a different Bible verse to drive at a deeper truth in order to untwist what has been twisted.

Jesus approaches Scripture holistically. When Jesus quotes the following to Satan:
"It is said, 'Do not put the Lord your God to the test",
he is not saying that Psalm 91 is untrue. He is stating that, without proper scriptural balance, Psalm 91 can be misunderstood and misused, even if used word for word.

Again, this is setting the stage for what is to come. It is a foretaste of what Jesus does, probably on a daily basis, in his ministry.

Back to the second part of Luke 4. *(You were beginning to wonder, huh?)*

Jesus enters his hometown synagogue and reads from Isaiah 61. This is a great, year of Jubilee, passage from Isaiah. It references a future time when God will set the record straight and place Israel back in its proper place of rule. It is the moment they had all been waiting for. They were ecstatic to hear the news that God was about to make all things right.

Then, like a good date that suddenly goes bad, they begin to question whether or not this guy they had known from his youth was really going to be the one through whom this prophecy would be fulfilled.

Did you catch that? Satan led every temptation with the statement, "If you truly are the son of God..."

Now, it is Jesus's audience who is wondering if Jesus is who he is claiming to be. When Jesus states in verse 21 that "today is the day" of fulfillment, he is making a claim as to who he is. The listeners are unconvinced.

Then, Jesus decides to make things worse. He juxtapositions two more stories, just like he had done before with Satan, alongside a passage they loved and for which they had longed for so terribly.

But they don't like his other Bible stories.
They don't like them at all.
Actually, they hated them. They especially
hated Jesus's use of these stories.

Jesus proceeds to tell the all-too-well-known
stories of Naaman the Syrian and the widow
of Zarephath. Both of these stories are about
tragic times in Israelite history when the
people really could have benefited from God
moving on their behalf.

With Naaman, the people of God had been
suffering losses in battle at the hands of the
Syrians. The military leader that is conquering
them is nonother than Naaman, a leper.

It is one thing to get conquered, but to be
beat by a leper just makes it that much worse!
What is God up to anyway?

Of all the people in all the towns in all the
world, God has the prophet Elisha heal this
man, a foreigner and enemy. The lepers in
Israel, well… they remained lepers.

The same is true of the foreign, alien widow.
During a famine, God sent Elijah to help her
and her son. And the widows in Israel, once
again, remained suffering during the famine.

Jesus uses the Bible to counteract
misunderstandings of the Bible.

It isn't that Isaiah was wrong. It isn't that Jubilee wasn't for Israel. It was that God was going to do something unexpected (*though perhaps it shouldn't have been unexpected*) with Jubilee.

Jubilee was about to go viral.
It was about to be for everyone. The poor and afflicted from any nation were about to be set free.

The oppressed of every people were about to be given freedom.

What the listeners had thought was only for them turned out to be for others. And they weren't happy. In fact, they tried to throw Jesus off a cliff. **Now that is some dedication to a particular understanding of Scripture!!!**

Notice what Jesus did in this story. He dismantled a current and popular understanding of Scripture with other story from Scripture.

Jesus did what Job had done with Eliphaz. The clear-cut, straightforward meaning of Jubilee got expanded by a better, fuller reading of the Bible.

And the idea that Jesus would be the one to bring this about, that ludicrous idea... well, it wasn't any more ridiculous than Israel's prophets being sent to foreign places to heal and provide for foreign people.

Jesus's listeners that day thought they had this whole life, Scripture and God thing all figured out. They thought they knew what God was going to do because they thought the Bible had told them what God would do. They thought that a "verse here" and a "verse there" approach was sufficient. They seemed to have missed the need to place different biblical stories side by side and allow them to interact with one another, allow them to interpret one another.

Who would have ever imagined that Elisha helping a widow in a foreign land would mean Jubilee was for everyone? It seems only Jesus knew that. Because only Jesus had taken the time, coupled it with wisdom, and let the two passages bounce off one another, bringing out a more complete meaning than can be arrived at with one passage alone.

Eliphaz's approach shuts out other information and clings to an old pattern and way of thinking. Eliphaz held tightly to presuppositions about the way life, Scripture and God work. Eliphaz wasn't alone. His way of thinking had permeated the minds of Israelites, all the way to the time of Jesus.

Sadly, his way of thinking is still prominent to this day.

But, it is time to say Goodbye to Eliphaz. It is time to recognize, as Jesus did, that Scripture is more complex than we might like to think. All of us like clear ideas and easily followable patterns. It makes life simpler.

But it fails to make life truer. And the simplest truth is that it isn't simple. It never has been.

Say goodbye to him before we do harm to the ones we love the most. The love Eliphaz surely felt for Job didn't stop him from being the worst friend in Job's life.

Say goodbye before we live a falsehood or partial truth because we haven't taken the time to consider God's word more fully.

Say goodbye before we take the teachings of Jesus and throw them over a cliff.

CHAPTER SEVEN

Jesus & Sabbath Clarity

Nothing, and I mean nothing, seemed to get under the skin of Jesus's opposition more than Sabbath contentions.

Eating and drinking with sinners. Yeah, his opposition didn't like it, but they could just call him a glutton and a drunk and move on, hoping others would soon see him for the tipsy, overeating man they believed him to be. Of course, the fact that the Bible states that rebellious children who deserve to be stoned to death are called "drunks and gluttons", might have something to do with why they like to describe Jesus in these terms.[54] It is also useful for them because these types of children are to be stoned to death...just what they wanted to do to Jesus.

"He is a rebellious child of God, refusing instruction.", they must have thought.

"We, his people, must do the right thing, follow the law and rid ourselves of this man ... permanently."

Hanging out with "them", those people, over there, who live in obvious disobedience to the ancient traditions and accepted ways... not

---

[54] Deuteronomy 21:18-21

super worrisome. Just call him their "friend", explaining away the easily visible success he appears to be having. It will soon die out as no one can build a movement with a group such as this.

But, when you start messing with Scripture and long-held beliefs as to how it works, how the passages and laws are to be interpreted and how they are to be applied... watch out! You are now poking the proverbial bear with a pointy object. The claws will come out, as we have already seen. Things are about to get messy.

I once sat in a Bible class and the discussion of Sabbath came up. One guy believed that Jesus deliberately went around, challenging the norms of Sabbath practice in order to cause much needed trouble. Another man stated that he didn't think he was quite so obnoxious, but that Jesus certainly didn't shy away from the Sabbath moments and traps. He would go in, full force, when needed.

Me... I'm not sure we can know if Jesus did things just to get under the skin of his opponents or if it is as the other gentleman recognized: Jesus never shied away from a

Sabbath confrontation. In fact, I am not sure it matters. The first opinion is possibly true. The latter is absolutely true.

Jesus never, as far as we can tell from the gospel accounts, backed down when it came to Sabbath laws and how they were understood and lived out. He never withdrew, thinking, "I had better not heal that guy... I might get in trouble."

No, he was pretty sure of himself when it came to the proper application of Sabbath ritual. It was as if he thought he was the Lord of the Sabbath or something!

His opponents were equally sure of what could and could not be done on the Sabbath. They didn't feel the need nor did they remotely have the desire to follow this Lord of the Sabbath.

And, this was a serious issue. Breaking the Sabbath wasn't some little sin with minor consequences. There wasn't a fine to be paid or a community service to be performed to make up for the infraction. As seen earlier, this is life and death. There is a lot hanging on getting this one right.

What we see in the life of Jesus is that, even though over a thousand years have passed since Moses received the law, no one seems to really understand how to follow it. There is simply too much ambiguity.

What qualified as "work" was the ambiguous question on the table. Answering that question proved difficult. Actually, it was basically impossible to say with certainty. But this truth didn't stop people from trying. And by trying, I do not mean a humble, lowly approach that recognized the ambiguity of the law.

The conclusions that were reached were serious lines in the sand that couldn't/shouldn't ever be crossed. Just read Numbers 15 if you think you can play loose with Sabbath laws. You'll think twice before you pick up sticks… or rub grains in your hands on the Sabbath.

Before we get into the story found in Luke 6 (and other Sabbath stories in the gospels), it is important to point out just what types of regulations had been built up around the concept of "no work". Because the law is so hard to pin down, and because the law carried the force of death if disobeyed, there was an obvious need to clarify what it meant to work. There was a need to differentiate between tasks that one must simply perform because one is alive and what tasks can wait or could be planned for ahead of time.

In the 5th century AD, the Jewish people had written down 39 restrictions regarding the Sabbath.[55] This document may reflect additions to what was thought during the time of Jesus and his dealing with the Jewish leaders of his day.

But what this document also does is shine light on the fact that there was nothing simple or easy about following this command to honor the Sabbath and keep it holy by doing no work. There were laws about bread making *(growing of plants, caring for them, harvesting them).* There were restrictions on the caring for garments and what activities could not be done. It speaks about the hides

---

[55] Orthodox Union
https://www.ou.org/holidays/shabbat/the_thirty_nine_categories_of_sabbath_work_prohibited_by_law/

of animals and even construction. The need for clarity was real.

Jesus ministry challenged the preconceived notions and long held traditions that had been in place and understood. In John chapter 5, Jesus heals a man who had been ill for 38 years. Jesus, upon healing the man, tells him to pick up his bed/mat and walk. Which, miraculously, the man does!

But there is a problem. This man is "carrying" something... ON THE SABBATH! The healed man is approached by the leadership and tells them the man who healed him told him to carry it *(sounds a little like Adam blaming Eve... just a little)*. But, he doesn't know who Jesus is. For now, Jesus is off the hook.

This bed carrying business, as it turns out, has been predetermined to be a breach of Sabbath code. Sticks... beds... what's the difference? Something was going to be done to this man, unless he could defer the consequence of his sin onto someone else.

Later on, Jesus finds the man in the temple. As soon as the man sees Jesus, he turns him in to the authorities.

They have an obvious reaction to Jesus. The reaction is to kill him, or at least start a plot by which he can be killed.[56] They probably longed for the good old days when they didn't need the authorization of the Romans to enforce their interpretations of the law.

This story shows us one of several restrictions that the Jewish people had put in place in an attempt to not break the Sabbath.

One more example before we get to Luke 6.

Luke 14:1-6, gives us another great example of restrictions and allowances that had been arrived at. Jesus, once again, shows himself to be Lord of the Sabbath by healing a man. Though I haven't read anywhere that states healing on the Sabbath is considered "work", it appears that it was definitely considered as such by the Jewish leaders.

Jesus, being watched like a kleptomaniac in a convenient store, sees a man who is in dire need of rest due to his suffering with edema,

---

[56] Later on in the story, Jesus makes things worse for himself by stating that his Father has been working this whole time, even NOW....on the Sabbath. He certainly didn't shy away.

a painful condition where fluid builds up around the joints and tissues in the body.

Apparently healing this man would be wrong; a clear violation of code.

But Jesus, upon healing him anyway, confronts them with what seems to be a Sabbath allowance they have made. He tells them that any of them, on the Sabbath, if they have a donkey or an ox that has fallen into a pit, would immediately pull that animal out of the pit.
Because it is the right thing to do!!!

Somehow, they had figured out that "work" of this type was acceptable.

"Put your stones down. Don't kill the man pulling a donkey out of a pit."

I show these examples to help give us insights into the complexity and near impossibility of following this law… or even knowing if you are doing it right or not. There was a recognized lack of clarity within the law that was being addressed for hundreds of years.

Back to Luke 6:1-5 and the Sabbath story found there.

Here, in what Luke has as the first Sabbath encounter, Jesus doesn't use their own conclusions against them as he does later in chapter 14. Nor does he immediately make matters worse by telling them that God is not at rest and that he is just like his Father.

In Luke 6, Jesus does what he had done with Satan in the wilderness. He does what he did with his neighbors and Nazareth community in the synagogue. Jesus uses Bible stories to clarify, amplify and modify other Bible stories.

In this story, Jesus's first activities that show a deep and misguided understanding of Sabbath is that of walking through a field, rubbing grains in his hands, and eating with his disciples.

Unlike healing on the day of rest, which can't be directly linked to a passage of Scripture, preparing food to eat on the Sabbath is a clear violation.

In Exodus 16, as God is giving the people manna from heaven. The text tells us that they are given by God 6 days of food for gathering, but that on the Sabbath, they are to stay indoors and not go out. Exodus 35 states that they can't even kindle a fire on the Sabbath, presumably for making food.

And here is Jesus, walking through a field and preparing food to eat.

Hasn't Jesus read the Bible?!! Doesn't he know what he is doing?

As an Eliphaz mindset might perceive the situation, the Bible is very clear about this type of activity. The actions of Jesus and his disciples are clearly wrong. Jesus needs to stop his rebellious ways and adhere to the law.

Except Jesus **has** read the scriptures. He **knows** the Sabbath passages and Sabbath stories.

What's more; he knows other stories as well. Stories that help to prioritize the passages of Scripture that seem, to many, to be so very straightforward.

Just as Jesus had done with those who sat and listened to him read Isaiah 61, Jesus juxtapositions a seemingly unrelated story from their history, putting it side by side with the passages they were clinging to in hopes of living in the blessings of Deuteronomy 28 and avoiding the never-ending curses.[57]

As the Pharisees *(now the worst thing a Christian could ever be called)* approach Jesus, they ask him why he is breaking the law.

Jesus answers, I like to imagine, with a somewhat sarcastic tone,

"Haven't you read your Bibles?!!!"

I am almost certain their immediate thought was, "Uh...yeah. We are the Pharisees. We are the ones in charge here. We are the ones who are in the know regarding the things of God. Who do you think you are? How dare you speak to us in this way!"

Though we haven't gotten there just yet, Jesus will soon tell them who he knows he is: He is the Lord of the Sabbath.

In a strange turn of events, Jesus continues his challenge that they simply do not read their Bibles. He tells them the story about the time David, as he is being persecuted by Saul, goes to the tabernacle and eats the

---

[57] Maybe if we do this thing right, God will eliminate Rome (enemies fall by our right had) and we will finally, once again, be the head and not the tail.

showbread that only the priests are allowed to eat.

Now, there is a lot going on here. Jesus has already, quite craftily I might add, insinuated at least 2 different things.

1.) He is like David, the rightful ruler.
2.) They are like Saul, the one who used to rule but whose days of leadership are coming to an end.

Jesus is also using the story to make a point about how we read and understand our Bibles.

Though it is possible to read a passage of Scripture, or even several related passages, and think our understandings are exactly as the Bible says, there are often other stories that will confront our presuppositions and challenge us to think again, even about the passages that seem to be clear.

David took the bread that, by law, was designated only for the priests. He wasn't allowed to do this. His action was a clear violation of what had been written down. It was in opposition to what Moses had heard God say to him.

And, yet, there David is. He and his men are enjoying a much-needed meal, seemingly thumbing their noses at the law of Moses.

Do you see what Jesus is doing?

He is adding layers of depth and meaning to a text that was once thought to be so clear.

Jesus does not, DOES NOT, simply toss the Bible to the side and say, "There's a new sheriff in town." To think Jesus does this is to simply ignore the gospels.

Jesus uses scripture to clarify, amplify and modify their misguided understandings.

The Pharisees and, to be honest, many of their constituents, viewed many passages as black and white. They are straightforward. And when they aren't as clear as they might have liked, they would do the work of making them straightforward.

And Jesus comes and shows them *(and us)* that we can't really approach life, Scripture and God this way.

Life is complicated and messy. Sometimes animals fall in old, dried-out wells and need rescuing. Sometimes people are sick and hurting and in need of help. Sometimes it is Saturday and you and your disciples are hungry and in need of sustenance.

What do we do when situations arise and make our decisions more difficult to determine? What do we do when laws collide and obvious right choices are hard to find?

What do we do when life doesn't make sense?

For those of us who love Scripture, we are presented with at least 2 options.

We can choose the path of Eliphaz and cling to our old patterns of thinking, or we can choose the path set out by Jesus. We can allow the Bible to serve more as a conversation with itself (putting two conflicting stories side-by-side) and pray and hope for the wisdom to know what the right thing is.

Speaking of old patterns, just before Jesus rubs those grains and eats, he talks about putting new wine in old wine skins and new patches on old clothes.

Jesus is offering a new way of thinking. He is the new wine and the new wine requires new wine skins. He is the new clothing.

The newness he brings to our understandings of life, Scripture and God are not totally different. He is not replacing old wine with water. The newness he brings is renewal, not replacement.

There are times in our lives when well-meaning people *(the Pharisees, I am certain, were well-meaning)* approach us, as Job's friends did, and hope to impart to us some easy fix to our problems. They often have some straightforward Scripture that they are certain will explain everything.

Mass shootings at our schools.
That is because we don't do publicly led prayers anymore.

Earthquakes kill and disrupt small islands.
That is because of pacts with the devil.

Hurricane Katrina hits Louisiana.
None other than Hal Lindsey has an explanation for that. God is judging America for its godless ways. Pat Robertson stated that God was punishing us for the abortions we sanction every year. Even the late, great Chuck Colson stated that he thought Katrina

was a warning from God that we need to defeat terrorists in a decisive fashion.[58]

I am not saying that God approves of abortion or that terrorism isn't a major concern. What I am saying is that it isn't so easy to connect the dots. Those who do are following the path and pattern set by Eliphaz and his friends.

Think about it:
Is God punishing us for abortion and other godless activities? Or is He warning us about the need to squash terrorism? These two things are not even remotely related to one another, and yet some of Christianity's most vocal and recognizable voices seem to have no problem declaring that they have pulled back the curtain and have seen the deeper issues at stake.

And they do so, based on the false belief that God is up to something predictable. He has allowed these tragedies to hit us, and the reasons are obvious.

---

[58]

https://www.mediamatters.org/research/2005/09/13/religious-conservatives-claim-katrina-was-gods/133804

But life isn't so easy.
Life is messy, rough around the edges and often impossible to understand.

Jesus, as he gives clarity to the *Sabbath (he actually seems to make the waters muddy as if that is how they are supposed to be)*, shows that simplistic readings of Scripture are often wrong-headed, no matter how well-meaning the people are who expound upon the events of life and their connection to Scripture and God.

So, we follow Jesus's lead.

We say Goodbye to Eliphaz and company. We bid farewell to that old way of understanding life, Scripture and God. We drink the new wine that Jesus brings. It is only appropriate that we do so.

CHAPTER EIGHT

Jesus, a Blind Man, Bloody
Sacrifices & Falling Towers

The idea that life is filled with easy answers and that those answers are found in Scripture isn't a new one.

Nor is it the case that a book like Job, as incredible as it is, was able to clear up the issue and make everyone realize that Eliphaz and his kind get it wrong, and get it wrong often.

No, this mindset and worldview existed when Job was written and endured all the way up to the times of Jesus. And, of course, it still exists today... or this book would be an utter waste of my time and yours.

Jesus dealt with people, and not just Pharisees and religious leaders, who seemed to always get it wrong. The idea that life, Scripture and God are easy to grasp permeated nearly every person Jesus encountered. Even his own disciples struggled with saying Goodbye to Eliphaz.

In Matthew 16:21-23, the Bible tells us that Jesus, from that time on, went around telling his disciples that he must suffer, be killed and then be raised on the third day. Peter, holding firmly to his preconceived idea of how this whole "Messiah" movement is supposed to work, *(based on his understanding of Scripture)* rebukes Jesus, telling him that this will never happen. In Peter's mind, there simply isn't any way these things are going to happen to Jesus.

But why wouldn't it happen?

Why does Peter get so hung up on this? So much so in fact that he **rebukes Jesus**[59], causing Jesus to say to him, "Satan, get behind me! You do not know the ways of God!"

The answer seems fairly clear. Peter has a vision, shaped by Scripture and his understanding of it, that simply won't allow Jesus to be killed and buried.

It seems Peter hasn't said Goodbye to Eliphaz. Peter isn't the only disciple keeping Eliphaz around.

In chapter 9 of the gospel of John, the disciples come upon a man who was born blind. They immediately assume, like that one guy we have been talking about[60], that this

---

[59] Can you imagine being the one who goes down in history as the disciple who rebuked Jesus?
[60] You remember Eliphaz, right?

man has obviously done something wrong... or maybe his parents. Either way, people are not born blind for no reason. Clearly there is a sin that has brought this Deuteronomic curse upon this man. It is also upon his family as he is unable to work and help.

Jesus assures them that their simplistic understandings of God and their sacred texts are incorrect. He heals the man.

As you might have guessed, if you didn't know already, Jesus heals him on... *dramatic pause*... the Sabbath. This is a double challenge from Jesus on why bad things happen and how we apply passages of Scripture to our lives when confronted with life's inexplicable tragedies.

Jesus, not backing down, tells the Jewish leaders that they are the people who are actually blind *(those who may be under a curse)*. After this event, and a few good teachings on Jesus as the good shepherd, we find the Jewish leaders with stones in hand, ready to eliminate this trouble maker.[61]

It appears that Jesus met Eliphaz everywhere he went.

One of my favorite stories of Jesus encountering Eliphaz happens in Luke 13.

Jesus is being informed about an incident that had occurred where Pilate had killed some Galileans and mixed their blood with the sacrifices that were being offered in the Temple. Based on Jesus's response, we see that part of that conversation with Jesus had to have been about **"why"**.

"Why did this happen? What sins did they commit? Just how bad were they? They must have been *really* bad, or this wouldn't have happened to them."

Jesus asks them a rhetorical question:

---

[61] Even Eliphaz wasn't that dedicated to his understandings!

"Do you think that because these Galileans suffered in this way that they were worse sinners than all other Galileans?"

In other words, this horrible event was being told to Jesus in hopes that he could reveal what great lawlessness these murdered people must have committed to deserve such a punishment.

Jesus, speaking rightly about life, Scripture and God, states that these Galileans weren't any worse than anyone else. It seems that sometimes, things just happen without reason. He doesn't explain it at all, nor does he attempt to.

He then brings up, all on his own, the story of the tower that fell in Siloam. 18 people died in that tragic event that loomed in the hearts and minds of the people of his day. He asks them the same question: *"Do you think this happened because they were worse sinners than the others living in Jerusalem?"*

The listeners would have previously thought that the answer was "yes". But Jesus tells them that it had nothing to do with their sinful state. Jesus offers no clarifying remarks. He doesn't explain the horrific

151

events that were seared on the hearts and minds of his listeners that day. He only warns them that things could and will get worse if people do not listen to him and change their ways.

Part of what Jesus does, time and time again, is confront the notion that life can be easily explained or that the plans and purposes of God are simple to grasp.

Life isn't easy.
Life is messy and rough around the edges.

And while an easy explanation is appealing, it simply doesn't, nor can it often, provide truth.

The idea that towers fall on really bad sinners may make you feel safe and secure the next time you are in a tower; but the truth is that it might very well fall on you. Perhaps this was part of Eliphaz's refusal to accept that Job had done nothing wrong. *"If he did nothing wrong and was suffering so greatly, then what is keeping me safe?"*

Jesus removes the clear understandings people often reach in life. It seems not everything happens for a reason, though everything that happens may have a lesson.

152

Jesus didn't say, "The tower fell on them so that you can learn an important lesson about repentance." Some may misconstrue this passage to say this, but it isn't so. Instead, Jesus uses something that happened for "no reason" to draw out a lesson.

As with the blind man in John 9, though the common understanding was that he or his parents had sinned and that that transgression was the cause of his suffering, Jesus takes the event a different direction. He takes it in a direction that they didn't, (or better still, **COULDN'T**), see coming.

Sin was not the cause of his blindness.

His parents weren't these god-awful people who had cursed their son, all the days of his life, by committing some atrocity... or by picking up sticks on a Saturday.

Much like Job and his ever-so-certain friends, there is something else going on that they are simply unaware of. Though it isn't a bet between God and Satan that is behind the scenes, there is another purpose that is beyond their ability to understand. God is about to do a work *(on a Sabbath)* and reveal once and for all, not just His power over sickness, but His ability to shine a light into the true darkness, revealing that those who see are blind and those that are blind can see.

This is not a conclusion Eliphaz can arrive at. He prefers to drink the old wine of explanation and wear the old garments of understanding. It feels safer there. He can explain everything there. But he is blind. He has entered into a rickety tower on the verge of collapse. He is about have his blood mingled with the sacrifices. He isn't safe at all.

Saying Goodbye to Eliphaz isn't easy. Letting go of our long-held and passionately-believed explanations is a struggle.

But it is a struggle that must be had.

It is okay to say we don't get it.
It is okay to recognize that sometimes things happen and the reasons, if there are any, are simply beyond our comprehension.

And it is okay to say that even the passages we always thought to be so clear perhaps are anything but.

Sabbath regulations seemed to be clear. God rested on the 7th day and commanded that His people do the same. And yet Jesus seems to muddy the waters a bit, making their understandings less understandable. And he uses Scripture to do it... which I love.

Jesus doesn't throw the Old Testament out, declaring it wrong from this point forward. Instead, he brings other biblical stories to the table, allowing them to reverberate off one another, creating new harmonies that weren't previously heard, but had been there all along.

Job sets the tone for this activity, giving the ancient Israelites an alternative way of understanding the sufferings they were experiencing.

This is a bit off the beaten path of this chapter, but just go with me down a small rabbit hole.

Imagine, for a moment, listening to the story of Job while in Babylonian exile. What that must have been like? On the one hand, you have the stories of 1 Samuel- 2 Kings rolling around in your head, pointing out the ungodly leadership that had seemingly brought about your captivity. Then a story like Job comes along and says that maybe it isn't so clear.

Maybe there is something else going on. And you are left to wrestle, like Jacob did, with God, with your thoughts and explanations, even the ones that come from Scripture.

Though I have been saying this all along, it bears repeating. Not everything can be explained in a nice and tidy fashion. Eliphaz doesn't have all the answers and often, his answers are completely off the mark.

The idea that earthquakes that killed as many as 300,000 people can be easily explained flies in the face of Job.

The idea that you can approach your own struggles and always find a sin that is directly connected to your bitter plight is wrong. You can't always do it. Often, connecting the line between sin and consequence is impossible because the "consequence" isn't connected to your sin.

Sometimes towers fall. Sometimes power-hungry leaders, bent on oppression and dominance, do violence to the innocent.

Sometimes people are born blind, and though there may be a lesson, there isn't a reason.

The Eliphaz part of our hearts and minds longs to clear everything up, compartmentalizing everything into nice little groupings. But Eliphaz was wrong. His friends were wrong.

CHAPTER NINE

Jesus & the "Need" for Violence

People have always loved their Bible stories.

For millennia, faithful followers have gravitated towards different events in the Bible, gathering up strength and courage to live as God's people. We look to our ancient, sacred texts to reveal to us who God is... who we are.

But as we have noticed, when we reflect too much on one passage and neglect others, we are bound to get it wrong.

As we noted in the last chapter, Peter seemed to struggle with this. *(As did the other disciples, albeit in a perhaps quieter fashion.)*

Peter seemed to believe, as others did, that whoever the Christ *(Messiah)* is, he is going to lead some sort of revolt, throwing out the evil empire that is oppressing the people of God, showing Himself to be the true king over all the world and empires of men. So, when Jesus says he is going to die, *(and saying this more than once)* ... it makes exactly **zero** sense. This kind of talk by Jesus needed to be repudiated, in Peter's opinion.

Peter's misunderstanding of just what it meant to be the Messiah and what it meant to follow the Messiah was what led him to rebuke Jesus.

This is why Jesus spoke to Peter and said "Satan, get behind me".

Even though Peter surely had passages of sacred text floating around his mind that led him to draw the conclusion that the Messiah must rule forever *(hard to do that when you are dead)*, he had somehow missed what Jesus said the Old Testament was about.[62]

At the end of Luke, after his resurrection, in chapter 24, Jesus tells 2 different groups of people that the Law, Prophets and Psalms foretold his suffering, death and resurrection. But they missed it. They hadn't been reading/hearing or understanding the whole story. They seemed to have been focused on certain passages of Scripture without understanding other passages. They hadn't taken the time to take stories of Syrian warriors, foreign widows and fleeing kings[63], and place them beside Jubilee passages and Sabbath regulations as Jesus had so creatively done.

---

[62] Daniel 7:9-14 among other verses
[63] Remember David as he ran from Saul.

As Luke tells us, their eyes had been closed to this truth, even though it had to be there all along.[64] It took a communion meal with Jesus for their eyes to be opened. Throughout Luke, Jesus indicates that a proper reading of Scripture would have allowed them to see.

It would have allowed them to see that the salvation of God was for everyone from every nation.

It would have allowed Peter and the others to see just what it meant to be the Messiah of God, that he must suffer, die and rise again.

It would have allowed the Jewish leaders to see what it really means to keep Sabbath.

In the end, everyone was blind.

There is a danger in restricting our beliefs about God to just a few passages, the ones we believe to speak "clearly" regarding certain situations and plans of God. Even though it seemed clear that Jesus, or whoever the Messiah was, **wasn't** going to die, Jesus retells the Old Testament stories, showing those two groups how much of the Bible they

---

[64] Luke 24:16

had misunderstood, or completely didn't see at all.

This seems to be true regarding the topic of biblical violence. After all, their ideas about violence and war against the enemies of God's people and their ideas about just what the Messiah would do go hand-in-hand. With the Messiah at the helm, the people of God would come to rule and reign as promised in the law.

But we know now, hindsight being what it is, that Jesus did none of those things. In fact, not only did he not do them, he seems to rebuke and condemn any thought that he might. Jesus seems diametrically opposed to violence.

How can Jesus, God's beloved son, Israel's true representative to God and God's presence incarnate, be opposed to something that, let's face it, the Old Testament seems to be in favor of? How can Jesus oppose violence when the Bible, his Bible, is filled with stories of God commanding violence and seeing fit to cause the enemies of His people to fall by the sword?

Now, it should be noted that for thousands of years, people have struggled with the violence found in the Bible. Especially the violence that is being commanded by God.

Commands to drive out the Canaanites and utterly destroy them as a way of dedicating the land to God are among many passages that come to mind.[65] Some of the stories and commands have led people, like Marcion of the late 1st and early 2nd century, to determine that the God of the Old Testament was a monstrous deity and Jesus defeated that God when he died and rose again. Marcion was wrong in his conclusion, but he was right to notice the struggles... which are real.

What do we do with a God that so clearly loves violence and bloodshed? Or is it so clear? Perhaps Jesus can help us understand who God truly is.[66]

---

[65] See Waltons' book, "The Lost World of the Israelite Conquest"

[66] I want to recognize at the outset that this chapter will by no means close the book on violence and the Bible. What I hope to show is that, though there are passages about violence, this does not mean these examples are to be emulated. Jesus, I believe, sets the record straight regarding this matter.

The gospel of Luke, my favorite gospel... I say this without guilt... tells us of a time when two disciples *(shockingly, Peter isn't one of them)* wish to call down fire from heaven to consume a people who have rejected the message of Jesus as Messiah. (Luke 9:51-56)

Before we get into Luke, we should take a look at the Old Testament stories that lie just under the surface of the Lukan account; informing the disciples of what they believe God should do next.

Where do they get this fire from heaven idea anyway?

The first story the disciples James and John, probably have in mind when thinking about this rebellious Samaritan village, was that of Elijah and the destruction of the prophets of Baal, found in 1 Kings 18. Oddly, this is the account of the events that occurred right after the healing of Naaman and the miraculous provision of the widow in Zarephath, the very stories Jesus uses to undermine their misconceptions about who Jubilee is for.[67]

---

[67] See chapter four of this book.

As the story goes, Jezebel had been killing off the true prophets of God as she led the people of Israel astray to worship the false god, Baal.

Elijah, one of the few true prophets left, finds himself in a confrontation with the false prophets of Baal. It is time for a showdown. There on Mount Carmel, God shows Himself to be the true God and Baal to be nothing but a total waste of worship - powerless, useless.

How does God do this?
He sends fire from heaven and consumes, in its entirety, a sacrifice that Elijah had prepared and had drenched in water for good measure. Like the magicians in Egypt, with Moses, the prophets of Baal couldn't do what God can do.

Then Elijah, in his victory over the false prophets and the false god, takes the defeated prophets down to the Brook Kishon and has them all killed.

BUT... this isn't the only fire from heaven story we find in the life of Elijah.

Just a few chapters later, in 2 Kings 1, we find yet one more fire-from-heaven story. And this one, while less known by many, is even harsher. It is also more than likely the main story James and John had in mind as they wished to call for fire from the sky. This is the last thing Elijah does before he is taken into heaven, not tasting death.[68]

In this account, Ahaziah, son of Ahab and Jezebel, falls through the lattice of his room and gets seriously injured. He wants to send some men to Ekron, to seek the counsel of the god Baal-Zebub, as to whether he will heal, or if he is a goner.

Elijah finds out what he is up to, stops the procession of men and has them send a message back to Ahaziah, asking why he would do this, given the fact that there is a prophet of God in Israel.

He also lets him know that Ahaziah's worst fears are about to come true. He is definitely a goner.

---

[68] You can see how a story like this might be both formative and memorable to the Jewish nation and Jesus' disciples.

Elijah goes, sits on a hill and waits. Ahaziah sends 2 groups of 50 men to Elijah. Each captain of the group calls Elijah a "man of God", to which Elijah says, "if this is true, may fire from heaven consume you all."

Both times they are consumed with fire from heaven. They have rejected God and his messenger, choosing Baal-Zebub of Ekron over the God of Israel.

A final, third group approaches Elijah, this time with the captain begging for his life. Elijah withholds the fire, but Ahaziah is still a goner. At least the messengers live to tell him he is going to die. *(A little silver lining there.)*

Now, in Luke 9, Jesus is making his way to Jerusalem. His disciples go ahead of him, attempting to prepare a place to stay for the rest of the disciples and Jesus when they arrive. Sadly, they are turned away once the residents of this Samaritan town learn that Jesus is just passing through and that his real destination is Jerusalem.

James and John, once realizing that these no-good Samaritans have rejected Jesus, the man of God, much like Jezebel or Ahaziah, immediately wish to reenact the fire from heaven scenes from Elijah's life.

Jesus will not have it. He rebukes them and tells them that he, the son of man, came to save, not destroy.

He rebukes them just as he rebuked Peter. They have missed the point. They hadn't in mind the things of God, but rather the things of man.

I must admit, when I first read this account from Luke while in college, my first reaction was to laugh.

I mean, seriously?!!

I thought it was funny that their first and immediate wish was to command fire from heaven to consume this city. It is just a bizarre thing to hope for, one that seems extremely exaggerated.

Who in their right mind would wish this?

What follower of Jesus would think that this is what should happen?

Perhaps stranger still is that they actually believed they could do it!

But just as we saw with the Sabbath laws and stories, it is easy for Bible readers to gravitate toward one story or understanding without considering other stories and passages that are vastly different than the particular story they might have in mind.

When the story of Elijah killing and consuming with fire any and all that oppose him and his God are the stories that form and shape you, you are setting yourself up to wish fire upon your enemies.

If your favorite Bible story is of the time when God broke out, killing His enemies with plagues, fires and crashing waters, it only makes sense that this is what you are going to hope to see in your own life and the lives of those around you.

James and John wanted to see God's power exhibited against the enemies of God. They wanted to see them fall by their right hand. When they asked Jesus if he thought they should call for a fire storm from the sky, they were certain (*probably*) that he would say, "yes... go for it!".

But instead, Jesus rebukes them, telling them that this isn't why he came. This type of thinking is opposed to the will of God.

But why does Jesus rebuke them?
What story or passages from the Bible does he have in mind as he corrects them?

This, unlike the other examples we have seen, is harder to pin down.

Jesus doesn't approach his disciples, reminding them of how God sent Jonah to Nineveh, capital city of Assyria, to offer them forgiveness. He doesn't tell them about how Jonah and his wish to see Nineveh destroyed was wrong and against the will of God. He could have. Reading this event from Luke, I think it would have been the perfect counter-story for his disciples to consider as they think about God's mercy and grace. If Jesus did share Jonah with them, we have no record of it.

What we do see is that Jesus stands opposed to the perceived need for violence that his disciples wished for, even though they have precedent for it; precedent from Scripture itself.

Here's another important thing to ponder:

Just previous to this event, Jesus tells his disciples, as they argue over which of them is the greatest, that greatness isn't what they think it is. Leading in God's kingdom is different than they had imagined. It means putting yourself last. It means to become like a child, one of the least influential, least powerful people to exist in this time of history.[69]

Jesus undermines, what was for the people of God, a common and easy-to-arrive-at conclusion that God will decimate any and all that stand opposed to him.

Leviticus 26:6-8 clearly states that God will make peace in the land and that the enemies of His people will fall by the sword.

Deuteronomy 28:7 tells us that the faithful will pursue their enemies.

The story of Elijah and others like it can powerfully inform a people as to what they believe God is going to do.

---

[69] Bock, Darrel L., Jesus According to the Scripture, Baker Academic, 2002, pg. 239-240

Why did Peter not understand that Jesus needed to die?
Well… Elijah didn't die. His enemies did. He was taken to heaven in a chariot of fire.

Why did the Samaritans deserve to die, being burned alive by a flame sent from the great beyond?

Because that is what Elijah did. That, they thought, is what God does.

Jesus makes it clear that this is not what he is about. He offers a correction to the idea that God needs violence to accomplish His goals.

The life of Jesus is filled with opportunities for him to utilize violence.

Jesus could have focused on stories of divine fire, famine and sword to direct his actions, but he doesn't.

Instead, he calls on his followers to love their enemies. Love the very people that their Scripture had promised would fall by their sword or flee from them in 7 directions.

He tells his followers to pray for those who are persecuting them.

He tells his disciples and his opposition, as they try to trap him, that they are to give to Caesar *(think Roman empire... think enemy)* his money/image back.

He tells them to walk two miles with the enemy.

He tells them to give them two articles of clothing when they only asked for one.

It seems that at every moment when Jesus could have acted like Elijah, he decides to act like Jesus instead.

With Eliphaz type clarity, everyone seemed to believe that God had a need for violence and that they, therefore, had a need for it as well. They seemed to know exactly what was happening and exactly what needed to be done in order to see the blessings of God and His victory flow.

But, like Eliphaz, they were wrong.

They didn't know.

They spoke wrongly.
(side note: you know you are speaking wrongly when Jesus looks at you and calls you "Satan" ... just saying)

What is clear is this: often in our clarity, we are blind.

The first group Jesus approached in Luke 24, Cleopas and his companion, believed that they knew what God was going to do. But, when Jesus died, they didn't doubt their understanding about life, Scripture and God,

They doubted Jesus. As they said in 24:21, "But we were hoping he was the one... ".

An Eliphaz approach is a blind approach. His eyes have been restrained and he cannot see. His certainty has blinded him.

But, as Jesus does time and time again, he takes the Scriptures and reframes them, putting them in a new perspective. He puts them in new wine skins.

Jesus doesn't toss out their stories but rather opens them so that they are more meaningful, not less. He removes the scales from their eyes, allowing them to see Scripture more fully.

May God remove the scales from our eyes as we say Goodbye to Eliphaz.

Violence in the Bible is a huge topic, and certainly not the focus of this book, but I have one more thought I would like to share regarding this. I will do so in the next chapter.

CHAPTER TEN

Jesus & the Cryptic Call for Peace

I love odd Bible moments. You know the kind.

Those moments that **don't make any sense.**

The stories that seem to be out of alignment with how we perceive and understand reality.

And let's face it, the Bible is full of stories that do this very thing. The sun standing still in the sky so battles can be won *(though, oddly, I actually do believe the sun remains still, but that is a different matter).*

King Saul finding a local necromancer to receive a message from the great beyond in hopes of getting some good news since God is eerily silent.

Genesis 38 tells us the story about a woman named Tamar who disguises herself as a prostitute in order to trick her father-in-law into having sex with her so she can have children. She does this because he has been withholding his son from her. Her plan works and he confesses she is more righteous than he is. A very peculiar story located in a very odd spot in the Bible *(It feels like it was just stuck right in the middle of the story regarding Joseph. Its location makes no sense to me.).*

Even the backdrop for this book, the foundation upon which this book stands, is an odd and wonderful story. Job's religious friends attacking him with their version of how the world works, backed by Scripture, only to find out they are wrong (*on second thought, this isn't really too far out*).

Yes, the Bible's pages are filled with intriguing accounts of events that baffle the mind. And I love those stories. They are part of who I am, even if I don't fully grasp their meaning at times.

Then, there is this one story found in Luke 22:35-38.

It is odd for sure, but not in the same way as the stories mentioned above. It is strange because, up until now, Jesus has sent out his followers to preach and teach without making provisions for what they will eat or what shoes they will wear.

But, things are about to change and Jesus knows it. The tides are turning and a great storm is mounting against Jesus and his followers.

It is here where Jesus tells his disciples to do the unheard of, at least unheard of as far as the commands of Jesus are concerned. He tells them to bring money and a bag. He tells them to sell their clothing, take the money and **go buy a sword.**

Here is the account:

35 He said to them, "When I sent you out without a purse, bag, or sandals, did you lack anything?" They said, "No, not a thing." 36 He said to them, "But now, the one who has a purse must take it, and likewise a bag. And the one who has no sword must sell his cloak and buy one. 37 For I tell you, this scripture must be fulfilled in me, 'And he was counted among the lawless'; and indeed, what is written about me is being fulfilled." 38 They said, "Lord, look, here are two swords." He replied, "It is enough."

But as strange as this turn of events is, it is about to get even stranger.

Jesus is on a mission to establish the kingdom of God "on earth as in heaven" (Lk 11:2). And now he has finally done what many, as we have just seen, had been hoping for all along. **"Let's get our swords and wage war."**

"Look, here are two swords!" his disciples exclaim.

Jesus responds with the most peculiar answer. ***"It is enough."***

"Uh...slow down there, Jesus. Let's not get **TOO** excited. Two swords **aren't** going to cut it. Not by a **LONG** shot. I mean, you can't do anything with two swords. You certainly can't turn over an empire with them. How can these possibly be enough?"

Then, as the story unfolds, it gets even more bizarre. Jesus is being arrested and Peter uses the sword, one of the two that Jesus had just told them to get, to cut off ear of the servant of the high priest *(he probably got overly eager and missed the real target... happens to the best of us)*. If ever there was a moment to use a sword, this had to be it! They were trying to bring Jesus in to the authorities and do who knows what to him. Whatever their plan is, Peter knows it isn't going to be pretty. After all, throughout Jesus's ministry, they have been trying to kill Jesus. Sitting idly by, *finally* with a sword in hand, just doesn't seem logical. I can hear Peter thinking to himself, *"This is why Jesus told us to get swords. It was for this moment. For such as time as this! Two swords are enough!!!"*

But Jesus heals the ear of Malchus, picking it up and putting it back on his *head (it is John who tells us it is Peter and gives the name of the servant)*.

This action by Jesus should give us pause. I am certain it gave Peter a reason to stop and wonder what was going on.

"Why in the world did Jesus tell us to gather swords if he had no intention of every using one?!!!"

Now, that is a great question.

First, I will do now what may ruin my fun later for any who know me and are reading this. I typically use this story, at least the part of Jesus telling his followers to get swords, as a way to pester my friends who are pacifists. Some have never seen this passage and are thrown into a state of confusion as they attempt to explain how Jesus would ever command such a thing.

But, this story isn't about Jesus telling his disciples to prepare for war. Jesus doesn't tell his followers to love their enemies one day and then, the next, tell them to take up arms and battle them to the death. Besides, two swords certainly aren't sufficient. And then rebuking your people at the first use of a sword... this is bound to confuse them.

So, why is this story here?

Well, I am sure it is here for more than one reason, but I would like to offer a reason that perhaps you haven't considered before. In order to do that, we need to consider one other story from Luke and then work towards connecting the dots.

In Luke 23:26ff, Jesus is being led away to be crucified. Peter's horrible swordplay and Jesus's healing of the servant's ear made sure that Jesus would be where he is; going where he is going. The powers of men, the empire of Rome, known for its violent and oppressive ways, has condemned Jesus to die on the cross.

As he makes his way to the place where he will soon die, Jesus is being followed by a great multitude of his disciples, the majority of whom are women. He tells them that things are bad and will get worse. He then says something so cryptic to the group that is following him that most of us will continue reading without giving much thought to what his words mean.

He says to them in verse 3, **"For if they do these things when the wood is green, what will happen when it is dry?"**[70]

What in the WORLD does that mean?

Let's think things through.

Jesus is leading a kingdom of God movement. But at this point, his movement is really no true threat at all to the Roman empire. It is like a fresh sapling with green wood offering no real threat to the all-powerful forest of Rome. Even Pilate sees this is true and tries to set Jesus free.

Jesus's movement isn't comprised of soldiers and fighters. It isn't made up of Israel's "best and brightest" or "those trained in war". Even their most ambitious and enthusiastic member can't swing a sword properly. And he is in possession of 50% of their swords!!!

As green as Jesus's tree is, as small a threat as he and his followers constitute, Rome will still crucify their leader for all in Jerusalem to see.

---

[70] NT Wright deals with this passage in "Simply Jesus", another great book. But you should finish reading this one first.

To paraphrase, Jesus says this:
"If this is how they treat a movement like mine, made up of fishermen and tax collectors who couldn't handle a sword to save their life, just imagine what they are going to do to your sons when they form an army of soldiers with thousands of swords. They will be utterly defeated, like a wildfire that rages through old, dry forests, they will be consumed."

Jesus understands that what is happening to him is only a foreshadowing of what will happen to all of Israel if they will not follow Jesus. This is why Jesus weeps over Jerusalem in Lk 19:41-44. This is why Jesus warns them in typical prophetic action, through the cleansing of the temple, of what is to come their way if they don't change in 19:45-48. This is why Jesus tells them to flee in 21:20-24.

And this is why two swords are enough. They aren't enough to defeat Rome. Besides, defeating Rome on the battlefield isn't what Jesus has in mind, even if the people think it is.

Just look at what Rome did to the leader of the group that possessed those two swords.

However, two swords are enough to show humanity that swords are not the way.

Violence and aggression are not the way forward.

Fire falling from the sky isn't what is needed, even though there are stories in our Bibles that make it seem that it is.

There is a better way.

And that better way is what Jesus came to show us and give us.

It is for this reason Jesus tells his disciples, and us, that being his true follower has nothing to do with fire from heaven or a consuming of the enemies of God.

Instead, Jesus says that being a part of his movement is quite the opposite. Soon after Peter declares Jesus to be the Messiah, Jesus tells them that being a follower of the Messiah entails denying oneself, picking up a cross and following him.

Two swords serve only to show the futility of swords and the violence they unleash.

As noted in the last chapter, the Eliphaz mindset might see things with crystal-like clarity, but the clarity is wrong.

Pat Robertson, while well-meaning and doing much good in raising funds to help those in need, still longs for an Eliphazic understanding of life, Scripture and God.

Peter and the others did the same.

If we are honest, we do too. But sometimes the things we think we understand turn out to be the very understandings we need to let go of.

Life is messy and hard.

Simplistic answers are troublesome, sometimes even harmful.

History's pages are filled with people who believed God had called them to military victory over the enemy. Many used (*or misused*) the stories from the Bible to back up their claims.

But Jesus turns those stories on their head. He redefines what it means to be great. He redefines what it means to be a child of God, living under the blessings and not the curse.

Consider these words from Jesus and watch how he turns Deuteronomy 28 on its head.

Blessed are the **poor**.

Blessed are the **hungry**.

Blessed are the **weepers**.

Blessed are the **hated**.

REJOICE!

BUT...

Woe to the **rich**.

Woe to the **full**.

Woe to the **laughers**.

Woe to the **well-spoken of and loved**.

MOURN AND WEEP!

These statements by Jesus go against the grain of his listener's understanding of how life and God work. It counters the accepted way of comprehending how the Scripture was applied to everyday life.

For Jesus, being poor was a blessing and being rich was a curse... a woe.

"Having enough" was a problem but "lacking" was a blessing.

Weeping and mourning were no longer the signs that indicated you were an unfaithful sinner.

Eliphaz got it wrong again.

Jesus tells us that these things are blessings, perhaps even signs that you are speaking rightly and living blamelessly.

Consider this:

As Paul noted in Galatians 3:13, dying on a tree is a part of the curse,[71] and yet Jesus, Messiah, son of God and establisher of the kingdom of heaven on earth, died on that tree. And he calls us to do the same.

While reconciling the differences between Jesus's attitude toward violence and that of the Old Testament is difficult, it seems clear that Jesus stood opposed to the violence of empires. He stands against the violence found in our communities and he stands against the hatred and violence between men and other men.

As Job did with Eliphaz, so Jesus does with his followers.

We may think we understand everything clearly, citing passages here and there that support our position, but sometimes it isn't that easy. Sometimes other Bible stories need to be considered to help balance out our thoughts and beliefs. Sometimes our own

---

[71] Deuteronomy 21:23

experiences contradict the way of thinking that we have for so long accepted.

And sometimes, Eliphaz is simply wrong. His understanding of life, Scripture and God are wrong.

It is time to put down our two swords and say Goodbye to Eliphaz.

Conclusion

A Prayer for Eliphaz

Much more could be said regarding Jesus and his creative use of Scripture.

We could look at how Jesus silenced the Sadducees by telling them that there is life after this life, otherwise the Bible wouldn't refer to "the God of Abraham, Isaac and Jacob" all the time. God is the God of the living, not the dead! This is pretty creative since these verses, in their context, say nothing about the current state of these departed people, but rather who they served when they were alive. But his logic shut them down.

We could look at his clever twist when asked about whether or not it is lawful to pay taxes to Caesar. He takes this opportunity to look at the "likeness and image" on the coin and compare/contrast it with the "likeness and image" on each person, the image that God made humanity in. Quite skillfully, he says to give to Caesar what is Caesar's and to God what is God's.

We could even look at the apostle Paul and see, in nearly every way imaginable, just how

197

much his encounter with Jesus changed how he viewed and used his sacred and ancient texts. As he said, everything he once held dear he counted as utter garbage and refuse.

His old ways of violence are behind him.

The zeal he once had has been redirected. He now knows that there are no groups of people who are his enemies. His war isn't against flesh and blood, but against the powers of darkness that exist just behind the evil power structures of human oppression and wickedness.[72]

Paul had drunk the new wine of Jesus and, in so doing, let go of the Eliphaz within him. His blind clarity drove him to persecute the church... persecute Jesus himself![73]

The examples are nearly endless, and we could go on, but I think what we have looked at in this book is sufficient.

---

[72] Ephesians 6
[73] Acts 9, Philippians 3

We know what needs to be done. Our attempts to make life make sense are more difficult than we know. Our simplistic understanding of just how the whole life, Scripture and God thing works has fallen short.

We know we can't and shouldn't blame earthquakes on pacts with the devil, as if that explains everything.

We know we can't attribute every calamity to some divine breakout of wrath as David did with Uzzah.

We know we can't see the suffering of those around us and do a spiritual connecting of the dots, finding the exact cause of what is happening.

But this hasn't stopped us from trying.

We watch the news and see school shootings and the Eliphaz within us (or among us) decides to make a post on Social Media about how this is all happening because prayer has been banned from school. If only prayer was

199

allowed, violence in schools would end. Sometimes our posts are even accompanied by a scriptural quotation!

Hurricanes strike our shores and we diligently try to determine just what ungodliness was happening in that place that would cause God to breakout in such a furious fashion. Again, finding an abomination in the stricken region is always helpful to explain God and His ways, especially if we really want to give a verse from the Bible... that way no one knows it is really just our opinion.

While this activity of finding the cause of every macro-misfortune may appear as silly to some, it is simply and horribly awful when done at the personal level.

Accusations of sin and guilt are made against a person who is hurting, struggling or sick. Especially if the "curses" never seem to go away... this is a clue that something has gone greatly wrong in their spiritual walk.

So, what do you do with Eliphaz?

What do you do when YOU are Eliphaz?

This is a wonderful question to ask, and it starts with acknowledging, even as Job did, that God is bigger than we are. God cannot be contained within our limited understandings. He is bigger. He is greater. Our attempts to explain Him, His plans and purposes are doomed to failure.

And, in Job 42, God hears Job's confession of His greatness and then God approaches Eliphaz. In this sense, He approaches us when we adopt an Eliphaz mindset and approach to life.

God tells Eliphaz that His wrath and anger have been kindled against him because he did not speak rightly about God.

As we have seen, Eliphaz only spoke about God what he understood the Bible to be saying.

"Doesn't the Bible say God blesses the faithful with good things and curses the unfaithful?", he must have thought.

"Isn't it obvious that the curses of God have fallen on this person, place or community due to their sinfulness and ungodly conduct?"

And yet Eliphaz, though backed by a multitude of passages from the Law and Psalms, spoke wrongly about who God is, how God works and how Scripture can be used to guide us through life. It was because of this that God was unhappy with Eliphaz and his two friends.

God then tells him what to do. He must make sacrifice, he and his friends, and then Job needed to pray for them. Job!!!

The one who suffered at their hands. The one who had been accused of dreadful and awful things. The one who was told that his children deserved to die. The one who was told that his suffering was nothing compared to the suffering he deserved.

It was Job who needed to pray for Eliphaz. God says that He will listen to Job's prayer and overlook their offense.

If you are Eliphaz, then you need to let go.
Let go of your overly simple and often harsh
understandings of life, Scripture and God.
You need to determine that a "verse here"
and a "passage there" understanding is
utterly insufficient when attempting to
explain the innerworkings of divine activity
and the interaction of this world with it.

Recognize that life is messy.
Realize that not everything can be explained.
In fact, a great many things in this life simply
defy logic and the explanatory efforts we
exhibit are futile.

Accept that towers fall on people for no
reason.
Accept that evil rulers will do what evil rulers
do... and they will do it to whom they wish.
The only thing that can be seen is the
wickedness of the ruler and his actions.
Nothing can be known of the state of the
people upon whom his fist of power fell.

Understand that sometimes, people are just
born blind. It is awful. It is sad. But it isn't a
sign of some punishment from the skies.

Know that life is messy, often with no reason
at all.

Learn that Scripture, while beautiful and from
God, isn't always as straightforward as we
might like… even the passages that seem to
be so are balanced against other passages, or
even experiences, in order to gain deeper
understandings.

Learn that God is beyond your limited
comprehension. And know that Jesus, while
being our clearest picture of who God is, still
doesn't make Him comprehensible. We still
see as in a mirror, dimly. But one day… not
today, but one day we will see clearly.

If you are Eliphaz, let go and enter the
mystery that is life. Enter into a world of
unknowns, a world where uncertainties are
acceptable. Embrace a way of living that says,
"I have no idea why those people died in that
tower or why those Galileans were killed by
Pilate.

I don't know why that man was born blind

I don't know what, if anything, caused that man to lose his family.

I don't know why that tornado hit that town.

I don't understand the paths of hurricanes and why some cities suffer from its power and others are spared.

**I. Don't. Know.**

Eliphaz made a sacrifice. He changed his ways. He asked Job for prayer.

If you are Job...

Of all involved, Job certainly has the toughest assignment of all. Pray for those who have hurt you, verbally assaulted you and accused you wrongly because they had a simpleminded understanding of this life, this Scripture and our God.

If you are Job, the one suffering at the hands of Eliphaz, you don't get to say goodbye.

You don't get to kick Eliphaz to the curb, declaring him unfit to be your friend or part of your life. Instead, God calls us to pray for them. This is especially true (and perhaps easier) after they have come to their senses.

It is tempting to send the Eliphaz among us packing, but Job doesn't end this way. The story ends with the restoration of all things. Yes, Job gets his possessions back. He has more children and is blessed. But he also gets his friends back, this time with a major dose of humility.

And so, we pray for Eliphaz. We pray for him to leave his simplistic understandings of life, Scripture and God behind and embrace the mystery of life as given us by God.

Because, in the end, we all have a little Eliphaz living in our brains, wishing to explain everything. We pray for ourselves that we can learn to speak rightly about God, as Job did. This is our prayer.

Bonus Chapter

If Job Wrote a Psalm

So much more could be said regarding the mindset of Eliphaz seen throughout the Bible. We could look at the book of Ecclesiastes, noting the unflinchingly harsh reality that the writer recognizes as part of life. The reality goes against the grain of Eliphaz's understanding of just how life works.

The author tells the sad tale of every human that has ever walked under the sun *(the land of the living)*. In this book, it seems that no matter how bad or good you are, in the end everyone suffers the same. All go to the land of darkness, never to return. The righteous, the wicked, the rich, the poor… it matters not. I think Eliphaz would have had something to say about this and, prior to his sacrifice and Job's prayer, would have had a thing or two to say to the writer of this powerful little book.

We could also look at the entire book of Psalms, noting the grand variety of thought and expression seen there.

There are some Psalms that Eliphaz would have been totally in love with. Psalm 1, for example, would have been a favorite. In it, the righteous always prosper. Even seasons of drought could not stop the blessings experienced by those who are faithful. In season and out of season, the righteous will bear fruit. The wicked, they will be blown away like dust in the wind. This sounds like simple, good doctrine to Eliphaz.

Be good, be blessed by God.
Be bad, be punished, maybe even destroyed, by God.

Yes, if Eliphaz were to write a Psalm, I am certain that Psalm 1 would have been the one to bear his name.

But, if Job were to write a Psalm, you can know that it would look and sound different from those that Eliphaz might gravitate towards. Maybe before Job's mighty fall from prosperity, he would have looked and acted more like Eliphaz, but during and after his ordeal, you know he thought differently.

There is one Psalm in particular that is very deserving of our consideration. It is one that I think Job could have written, had he written anything down.[74]

This Psalm is brutally honest, much like Ecclesiastes, with the reality of life. It stares old patterns and ways of thinking in the eyes, holding up the experience of real life in the face of Scripture, asking tough questions that don't seem to get answered.

Yes, if Job had written a Psalm, it would have been this one.

Psalm 44 is only 26 verses long, but makes the point that we have been striving at this entire book.

It starts as many Psalms do, with what seems to be a fond remembrance of how good things used to be. The Psalmist remembers when God drove out the enemies of Israel, giving them the promised land of Canaan. He remembers the plucking God did of the

---

[74] Job 19:23

nations and the planting He did of Israel in that good place. And He did this because He favored them.

The song writer even seems to express a great faith that God will do for them what He did for their ancestors. Through God, they will destroy their enemies, putting them to shame.
SELAH...

But, right about verse 9, things get messy.

Quite unexpectedly, the Psalmist states something about God that just shouldn't be! He has forsaken them.
He has cast them off.
He has put them to shame.

No longer does God go out with the warriors, giving them victory over their foes. Instead, they are turned back. The enemy sweeps in and destroys them. The enemy takes the plunder.

Verse 11 states that God has turned them into food for the enemy, like sheep they are scattered. Verse 12 isn't any better. God has sold them for next to nothing. The Psalmist says that this was done to show just how worthless they are in the eyes of God. The experiences of this Psalmist, much like those of Job, are reminiscent of the curses found in Deuteronomy 28. And, we all know that these curses are caused by one thing and one thing only.

NOW STOP.

If you were reading the Psalm, stop at verse 16.

If Eliphaz were reading this, like a letter Job had written down for Eliphaz to consider, he probably already has an answer to the woes being experienced by this biblical author. The reason they are not being treated by God in the same fashion as their ancestors is simple. The blessings have gone and the curses have come, and the reason why is pretty obvious to Eliphaz.

Clearly, they have sinned.

They have gone astray, forgetting God and His ordinances. Somewhere along they line, it is plain to see that author *(or Israel as a whole)* has messed up royally, otherwise their enemies would rise only to meet their destruction. They would be scattered in 7 directions, leaving Israel to enjoy the spoils of war, just as the Bible says.

Before we get to verse 17, I believe that Eliphaz would have jumped in with his easy to understand, easy to grasp explanations of life, Scripture and God. He would have stopped reading the letter, looked the author in the eye and reminded them of just what Psalm 1 says, just so this Psalm 44 guy would know what is really going on.

And to him, the Psalmist who wrote chapter 44 would say:

"All this has come upon us,
   *yet **we have not forgotten you,***
   or been false to your covenant.
*18 **Our heart has not turned back,***

nor have our steps departed from your way,
¹⁹ yet you have broken us in the haunt of jackals,
and covered us with deep darkness.

²⁰ If we had forgotten the name of our God,
or spread out our hands to a strange god,
²¹ would not God discover this?
For he knows the secrets of the heart.
²² Because of you we are being killed all day long,
and accounted as sheep for the slaughter."
(NRSV)

The Psalmist seems to be all too familiar with the way Eliphaz thinks. It seems more than likely that the Psalmist once thought about life in the same way.

But, like Job, reality contradicts passages of Scripture like Psalm 1 and Deuteronomy 28. And the author refuses to change their perception of reality in order to make the Bible behave they way they think it should behave.

The Psalmist doesn't start to invent faithless acts in order to repent and get back on track.

The Psalmist declares that something isn't right. If they had sinned or been unfaithful, God would know it and it would be pointless to declare that they are innocent, but the writer knows that they have not turned back nor have they forgotten God *(the very thing Deuteronomy states will happen, causing the curses to flow)*. Instead, it seems that God has fallen asleep at the wheel of their lives, causing them to fall victim to the curse, even though they don't deserve it.

And, as you have suspected, the Psalmist ends, like Job, clinging to God while living at the ragged edge of death, bodies clinging to the dust as if on the verge of taking their last breath. Both Job and the Psalmist can't do anything but rely on the mercy of God to come and rescue them from their trouble.

Psalm 44 stands in contrast to Psalm 1. It recognizes that Psalm 1, while sometimes true, isn't always true. And it fearlessly stands before God and calls Him to account for the pain, suffering and loss that they are experiencing undeservedly.

Eliphaz reads only Psalm 1 and others like it.

Job reads Psalm 1 and balances it, perhaps even counters it, with Psalm 44.

Both are in the Bible.

Sometimes, much to our dislike, life doesn't make sense. Our simple explanations fall short and our abridged knowledge of Scripture fails us.

Eliphaz cannot deal with reality and will quickly accuse even one of the most righteous men who has ever walked the face of the earth of egregious sins and acts before he will change his perception of life, Scripture and God.

And this is one of the many things that makes the Bible so exciting. It offers black-and-white solutions while at the same time recognizing that often these solutions fall so terribly short of giving us the answers we so desperately seek. They even fall short of speaking rightly about God.

As has been stated at the end of every chapter of this book, it is time to say Goodbye to Eliphaz. Or, perhaps a better way of saying it, it is time for Eliphaz to make a sacrifice and have Job say a prayer for him. It is time for Eliphaz to repent, change his proud and arrogant ways and humbly admit that sometimes, there are no easy answers.

Often, there are just questions that defy explanation. Often life slaps us in the face without cause and without reason. God tells us, in Job, Psalm 44 and in the life and ministry of Jesus, that it is okay to not know the answers. It is okay to weep and cry out to God in hopes that He is listening.

Perhaps counter to your belief, behaving this way is an act of faith, not an act of rebellion. Doubts and fears are okay. Not knowing the answer is okay. Not only is it okay, it is a positive in the life of the one who seeks God's face.

So, struggle with God. Wrestle with Him. You can because you have said Goodbye to Eliphaz

and are living a life of true, deep and real
faithfulness to God.

YOUR LUCKY DAY!!!

More Books by Rob Coyle

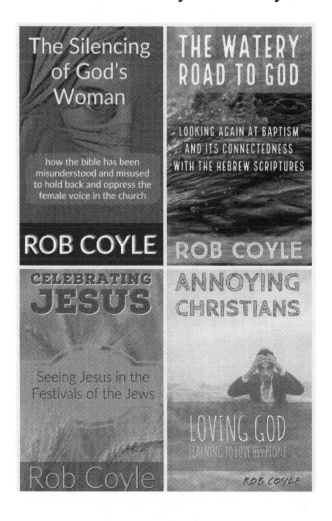